# More advance praise for
## *Where Can Mom Live?*

"This is an unbeatable combination of superior conceptual and technical knowledge with a wonderfully readable style. The book describes various elderly housing options with enough richness of detail to visualize how they work. *Where Can Mom Live?* combines the expert knowledge of geronotologist Vivian Carlin with the finely crafted phrases of writer Ruth Mansberg." —*Daniel A. Quirk, Ph.D.*, Executive Director, National Association of State Units on Aging

———

"The authors communicate clearly the basic fact that housing is more than a roof over one's head. It is a supportive living environment whose purpose is to maintain a person's preferred lifestyle while safeguarding health and independence for as long as possible. They recognize that when a family exists, living arrangements should be a family decision. The book is a practical guide for family members and the older person. It may be especially helpful to older persons without family members in that the advantages and disadvantages of various types of housing arrangements are so clearly illuminated." —*Lennie-Marie P. Tolliver, Ph.D.*, University of Oklahoma School of Social Work, former U.S. Commissioner on Aging

———

"The family in a quandry will obtain help from the exposure to the actual decision-making process that the families depicted in this book had been through. I recommend it highly both for its informational content and for the book's willingness to discuss the positives and negatives that different older people with differing needs have found in various housing alternatives." —*M. Powell Lawton, Ph.D.*, Director of Research, Philadelphia Geriatric Center and past president of the Gerontological Society of America.

# Where Can Mom Live?

## A Family Guide to Living Arrangements for Elderly Parents

by

### VIVIAN F. CARLIN, Ph.D.
### RUTH MANSBERG

Lexington Books

D.C. Heath and Company • Lexington, Massachusetts • Toronto

Carlin, Vivian F., 1919–
Where can mom live?

Includes index.

1. Aged—United States—Dwellings.   2. Parents, Aged—Care—United
States.   I. Mansberg, Ruth,
1924–    . II. Title.
HD7287.92.U54C37   1987        363.5′9        86-45526
ISBN 0-669-13665-4
ISBN 0-669-13666-2 (pbk. : alk. paper)

Published simultaneously in Canada
Printed in the United States of America
Casebound International Standard Book Number: 0-669-13665-4
Paperbound International Standard Book Number: 0-669-13666-2
Library of Congress Catalog Card Number: 86-45526

The paper used in this publication meets
the minimum requirements of American National Standard
for Information Sciences—Permanence of Paper
for Printed Library Materials, ANSI Z39.48-1984.

ISBN 0-669-13666-2

87  88  89  90   8  7  6  5  4  3  2  1

*To older people living in new and innovative housing arrangements. Though still few in number, they are blazing trails for the rest of us.*

# Contents

# Acknowledgments

W E thank the staff and residents of the following housing facilities, housing programs, and social agencies who gave so generously of their time: The Cottage Place, Elm Court, HAREL Program (Daughters of Israel Geriatric Center), Kirkside at North Branch, Navesink House, Kittay House, Share-A-Home Inc., Housing Authority of Bergen County Elderly Conversion Home Options, Mercer County Outreach Program, COPSA—Shelter Clearinghouse, Housing Coalition of Middlesex County Home Match Program, Princeton Senior Resource Center, Jewish Family Service of Delaware County, Older Adult Resources and Services (OARS), Warren County Housing Programs, and The Equitable Life Insurance Society of the United States.

In addition, we thank the many sons, daughters, and mothers who shared their experiences with us—particularly the two who were models for our key story of Edna and Carol.

Their help was indispensable in the creation of this book, which, we hope, will serve you well as a guide to making wise housing decisions.

# Introduction

GROWING old today offers more possibilities for the good life than ever before. It also brings with it some very tough questions. After health, the most difficult of these involves housing. Often the first depends on the second: where the elderly live can affect their well-being as much as what they eat. And living alone in old age can be hazardous to their health.

When problems do arise, who bears the brunt? Usually it is an adult child. This can happen at a time of life when middle-agers face many problems of their own—the empty nest (often with lingering dependents somewhere out there), career decisions, preparation for retirement, or possibly marriage and health problems.

This book speaks to those of you who have aging relatives and are searching for solutions to their housing problems. The pressure on you is growing. Many of your parents who moved to sunny climes at retirement a decade or two ago now need long-distance attention or are returning to live with you.

Your generation, now coming to maturity, is faced with the responsibility of caring for aged parents in unprecedented numbers. The fastest-growing age group in the United States is 65 and older, over 11 percent of the 1985 population. (At the beginning of the century, this group was only 4 percent of the population.) Of this 65-plus segment, 38 percent is 75 years and older and accounts for 5 percent of the total U.S. population, a figure that is expected to double in less than half a century.[1]

---

The characters, life sketches, and places described in this book are based on real people and places but have been modified and given fictitious names to protect their privacy.

No wonder, then, that the subject of aging parents comes up so frequently in any group of people over the age of 40. Let one person mention a hardship with an elderly parent, and at least four out of five others will join in with talk of similar problems. Sadly, these conversations sometimes convey the impression that longevity is a curse rather than a blessing.

Yet we know that the majority of elderly not only live independently, but prefer to do so, and that there is as wide a range of ability, talent, and lifestyle among the old as among the young. Aging only accentuates the individuality developed over a lifetime. Some common threads, however, do run through the aging process, becoming more predominant the older we get. Physical changes occur, such as hearing and vision losses, decreased muscle strength and agility, and increased sensitivity to extremes of heat and cold.

Physical frailties, in turn, can and often do lead to psychological and social changes. The life circle, already reduced by retirement and the departure and death of family members and friends, shrinks still further. Mobility is curtailed, and more and more time is spent at home. At the same time, changes in the surrounding neighborhood may aggravate fears for personal safety and the difficulties of shopping and socializing.

Stories abound of lonely old people who become depressed and neglect themselves and their homes, disregarding even basic hygiene and nutrition. This often leads to cycles of illness and deepening despair.

Depression in the elderly can be brought on by an illness, by the illness or death of a dear friend or relative, by declining mobility, by being the victim of an accident or theft, by the adverse effects of medication, by poor nutrition, and so on. A friend told us that his 77-year-old widowed mother stopped shopping after her wallet was lost or stolen from her handbag for the third time in two years. "Until then, shopping was one of Mom's favorite pastimes," he explained. "Part of the problem was absent-mindedness. She'd forget to close her handbag. After a while, her confidence was completely eroded. Now she rarely leaves home."

Others tell of parents who cope with their loneliness in ways that eventually defeat them. Collectors go wild and end up living in houses that resemble junkyards, patients who have outlived their doctors are still taking pills prescribed years before, and mournful-looking people haunt doctors' offices and wait hours to speak to a physician for a few minutes.

"Poor old thing, she's getting senile," is a common response to such eccentric behavior. Maybe she is and maybe she isn't. Until quite recently, senility was thought to be a normal part of aging. But recent research disproves this. Instead, we are learning, normal aging need not mean mental dysfunction. Such impairment often can be traced to a specific disease, to overmedication, or to a nutritional deficiency.

Much more remains to be learned. Society was not prepared for the population explosion among our top age groups; consequently, much of the territory is still unexplored. The elderly themselves, most of whose parents died by age 60, have few role models in their own past to fall back on. Early in this century, life expectancy at birth was 49 years; today, it is close to 75 years. But men who survive to age 65 can now expect to live another 14 and one-half years; women can expect almost 19 more years. Because of this difference in life expectancy, the ratio of men to women drops steadily throughout later life: from 80 men per 100 women at age 65 to 42 men per 100 women at age 85. The dwindling number of men and the tendency of older men to marry younger women accounts for the large numbers of women who live alone. At age 75, for example, 70 percent of the male population is married, while over 70 percent of the women are widowed.[2]

For the most part, these elderly people are our mothers and grandmothers. They are also our fathers and grandfathers, but the male elderly are fewer in number. Because the reality is that many more women than men need the kind of help offered in this book, we have used feminine nouns and pronouns throughout. But there is no reason why the advice cannot apply to male relatives as well. (In general, older widowed men living alone are at greater risk because many were accustomed to having their wives take care of their personal and social needs.) Even older couples who are doing poorly on their own can benefit from some of our suggestions.

Whether mother, father, beloved aunt, or friend, remembering their roles in our lives we will not abandon them. Though they may live far from us, we keep in touch and are on call in times of trouble. The 80-year-old widow, who trips on a loose floor tile in her kitchen in Miami and is hospitalized with a broken leg, is soon on the phone to her daughter in Boston, who flies down and is at her bedside the next day. (At what cost and inconvenience, only the daughter and her family know.) When Mom returns to her apartment, arrangements must be made for full-time care. Because her recovery is slow, she feels confined and bored. Months later, though the leg is healed, she is clumsy and fearful of walking and rarely goes out. A few friends still visit, but she is lonely and increasingly depressed. The daughter, who visits as often as she can, suggests that Mom give up the apartment and come to Boston to live with her and her husband.

This story, with minor variations, is commonplace. Accidents are among the leading causes of morbidity and death for the elderly, and most of them occur around the home. And when they do occur or when illness strikes, many families think the only alternatives are either to have the relative move in with them or to mount a valiant struggle to keep her in her own home. The first arrangement is bound to foster greater dependency; in addition, it may create troublesome intergenerational conflicts. And helping this relative stay in her own home may or may not be worth the effort, depending upon whether living conditions can be improved and whether opportunities for socializing are available.

Actually, no one ought to wait until an accident or illness happens to an aging relative. It could be the beginning of a downward spiral that results in an irreversible decline. Home is extremely important to older people because they spend so much time there. In addition, we believe that physical and mental decline in old age are often the result of an individual's home environment. (This is probably true at any age, but older people have less resilience than younger ones.) It hardly needs saying that home should be safe, clean, comfortable, and convenient. It should also be affordable. Many of our elderly live on low fixed incomes and pay a disproportionate amount for shelter; the average is about 40 percent of income, but some spend as much as 70 and 80 percent—virtually starving themselves to keep a roof overhead.

When living conditions are unsafe or unsanitary, isolated or lonely, the caring person will want to help improve the environment or to find a new and better one for the older person. The aim of this book is to help the helpers. We will tell you how other people searched for and found housing solutions for their aging relatives, describe a variety of possible living arrangements, and alert you to the emotional and practical pitfalls involved in moving some older people to new housing or in persuading them to make needed changes in their present homes.

Our major focus will be on house or apartment sharing, shared group homes, and congregate and life-care communities. But we will also touch on other alternatives, such as living with adult children, retirement villages, residential hotels, elder cottages, and board-and-care homes. For those older people who stay in their own homes, we will suggest ideas for financial, physical, and social improvements: measures such as home-equity conversion, safety features, house sharing, and accessory apartments.

To help you and your mom evaluate her needs and lifestyle preferences, you can use the checklists in chapter 7. The answers will serve as guides to making intelligent housing choices. You will also find specific advice on where to go for more information and assistance once your mother has made her choice, a checklist of what to look for during a housing search, and a checklist on safety and convenience features in the home.

By the time you finish this book, you will be informed about many of the psychological, social, humanistic, and economic aspects of alternative living arrangements that are proving beneficial to many old people. You will have learned about the parts played by personality, attitude, and physical condition in the process of aging—especially as they relate to the strong attachment to home—and about ways to overcome resistance to change. You will also be alerted to the importance of not waiting too long before helping your parent plan a move. This information should come in handy when it comes time to persuade, cajole, or lobby your elderly parent concerning the necessity for making some changes in her life.

Once that's done, you should be able to make good use of all the practical advice on how to help an older person develop a new life plan, how to find and evaluate housing, and what legal and financial factors to consider. By matching available living arrangements to her needs, preferences, and functional abilities, you and your mother should be able to make the best possible housing choice.

Through it all, remember this: as we age, we all experience some physical, economic, psychological, and social changes. These must be taken into account in the housing choices you and your parents make together. The elderly's housing needs are different in many ways from those of younger families. Depending on location of the housing, health status of the individual, availability of services, and access to transportation, a house or apartment can unintentionally become a kind of prison. So the simple provision of shelter is not enough. Housing should provide a living environment that will allow the person to continue her preferred lifestyle, while at the same time safeguarding her health and independence for as long as possible.

It's well to remember, too, that all of us—if we live long enough—are going to need some help from family and community. We sincerely hope this book will serve you well in helping someone you love.

# 1

# One Widow's Dilemma

FAMILIES aren't what they used to be. Perhaps they never were—at least not in the 20th century with its swift, revolutionary changes in technology and mores. This century's increasing urbanization and the quest for more material possessions diminished the desire for large families, and the availability of birth-control devices made smaller families possible. Young adults, escaping from the agrarian drudgery of their parents and grandparents, no longer felt the need to populate the farm with children to insure its survival and to provide for their care in illness and old age.

The close-knit societies of rural villages and small towns gave way to cities and, after World War II, to their suburban extensions, where anonymity, privacy, and mobility were (and still are) zealously guarded. Families shrank to mother, father, and one, two, or three children—whatever the young couple thought they could afford. Planned parenthood became the order of the day.

Much of this is changing still. Families are being fractured, fragmented into one-parent, childless, and changeable-mate units. Undoubtedly, these patterns also will shift and reshift. Where and how do our growing numbers of old people fit into this kaleidoscopic picture?

One of the fundamental changes of this century has been an increased lifespan for more people. There are more than 28 million people age 65 or older living in the United States today—almost 12 percent of the population, as compared with the barely 4 percent this age group constituted at the beginning of the century.[1]

A young person in the early 1900s might have hoped to live into his or her 70s or 80s, but the odds were very poor. Life expectancy at birth was 49 years. Women who survived their childbearing years died at about the same age as their husbands. A child born in 1984 could expect to live 74.7 years; a woman who reached the age of 65 in that year could expect to live another 18.7 years, a man another 14.5 years.[2]

Advances in medicine, pharmacy, and nutrition have been spectacular. Life is preserved and prolonged by an astonishing variety of pharmaceuticals—antibiotics, antitoxins, tranquilizers, and diuretics; apparatus such as pacemakers, dialysis machines, and heart-lung machines; sophisticated surgical techniques—heart, intestinal, and prosthetic; and supermarkets stuffed with proteins, carbohydrates, vitamins, minerals, and assorted additives to prevent food spoilage and improve its color and flavor.

Beyond physical preservation, there are the psychological lures to long life: increased travel possibilities and conveniences, proliferation of cultural and sports facilities (colleges, museums, concerts, opera and ballet companies, race tracks, gambling parlors, stadiums) and, most important of all, television. The poorest elderly shut-in with a TV set will drag through one day after another to see what happens in the next episode of a favorite soap opera. All the glitter, glamor, violence, and romance of the world now enter even the drabbest room via the flickering tube.

How is this increased longevity affecting family life? No doubt it is creating some problems. But for the most part, families that maintain ties with their older generations are rewarded and enriched by generous gifts of love and experience. And no matter how much fracturing and restructuring a family undergoes, an elder can usually count on at least one younger relative in time of crisis.

For Edna B——, it was her daughter Carol. Carol, her husband, Bert, and their two sons may be characterized as a typical suburban nuclear family. Unlike many of her peers, however, Carol stepped out of the housewife role and resumed her career as an architectural designer as soon as her younger son entered first grade.

The most pronounced impression on meeting this mother and daughter was the closeness of their relationship. It aroused the envy of many of their friends.

"Edna and I have been good friends all my adult life. Though I did give her a hard time when I was a teenager," Carol said.

"That's all right, dear," Edna retorted, "I'm getting back at you now. Now I give you a hard time."

Carol shook her head in silent denial. But later, when Edna had gone off to make tea, she acknowledged the subtle change in their roles. "I don't know when it happened. Probably because it didn't happen all at once. But sometime in the past year or two, Mother has become more the child and I more like the mother."

Thoughtfully, Carol traced the beginning of this reversal to the period when Edna's cataracts, despite several operations, caused so much loss of vision that she had to give up driving. That meant Edna was completely dependent on others for rides to meetings, doctors' appointments, the bank, and the supermarket. After a while, all but a few friends stopped offering. Edna was reluctant to ask, and as a result spent more time alone in her apartment.

"Mother's a very social being, and this was very destructive to her. She began to lose interest in dressing and eating. I'd come up in the evening after work with a bag full of groceries and find burned pots and kettles that she'd left on the stove and forgotten while absorbed in a news program or discussion. She'd still be in her robe and slippers, too. Often she couldn't remember whether or not she had taken her medication that day."

To understand this decline, you would have to have known Edna in her prime—an intelligent, vibrant woman, active in her community. Shortly after their marriage, she and her husband had bought a house in the small Long Island town where Edna grew up. They lived there for 34 years. Here, Carol and her younger sister (who later settled in Colorado) grew up. After college and marriage, Carol moved into a house in the same town; she and Bert rented at first, then bought a three-bedroom house about one-half mile from her parents' home.

Carol joined some of the same organizations that Edna belonged to: the local League of Women Voters, a group calling itself "Improve Our Schools," and ad hoc environmental committees to protect the purity of water and air. They were a familiar pair at town council, zoning board, and planning board meetings, usually supporting each other's positions.

At about the time Carol went back to work for a regional architectural firm, Edna became president of the local League of Women

Voters. A few years later, she won a seat on the school district's board of education, a seat she held onto through four elections until she resigned. During these years, she also studied psychology and languages at a nearby college and regularly played tennis and bridge. Carol joined her for a tennis game whenever she could. "She was a ferocious player," Carol said, only half-joking. "It took years before I learned how to beat her."

Just after their 34th wedding anniversary, Edna's husband died suddenly. No previous illness had prepared his family for the shock. "It was a terrible blow to all of us," Carol reflected sadly. "But Edna was only 58, still relatively young, and seemed to recover pretty well. All our friends admired her for picking up the pieces and getting on with her life. I know how much she missed my dad—still does, but I doubt many of her friends suspected.

"Anyway, afterwards she threw herself into more activities than ever before—more courses, more meetings. She even ran for town council on the minority-party ticket. Came pretty close to winning, too. And she did a lot of traveling in the first few years."

Two years after her husband died, Edna sold her house and moved into a two-bedroom garden apartment in town. Carol was uncertain at the time that this was a good decision. But Edna insisted: "I don't like rattling around in this big house with all the ghosts of yesteryear. And it takes too much of my time and energy to keep it the way it should be kept." Carol, Bert, and the boys helped with the move.

And indeed, Edna seemed more cheerful once she had settled into the apartment. "But there was an underlying restlessness. She was always on the go. Spent very little time at the apartment—or here, for that matter, though Bert is friendly and the boys adore her. I saw more of her at meetings and at parties with mutual friends," Carol said, adding that they shared many of the same friends.

Seeing mother and daughter together, an observer would be struck by the physical resemblance, despite the 23-year difference in their ages. Though Carol had softer, prettier features, they both had the same bold blue eyes, the same way of tilting their head with a half smile when listening or pausing to think, the same quick, forceful manner of speaking. Both were tall, slim, and erect (Edna remarkably so for a woman of 78 years), as if they practiced for perfect posture. But Edna's white hair, lined, craggy face, and thick eyeglass lenses bore witness to her age.

Our first conversations took place in Carol's home, a comfortable, two-story frame house on a tree-lined street. Edna was finishing a three-week convalescent stay after a bout of pneumonia had sent her to the hospital the previous month.

"I feel like Jimmy Durante—I don't know whether I wanna go or I wanna stay," Edna joked. "Not quite true, of course. I definitely don't want to make this my permanent home. My mother lived with me for most of my married life. And she lived to be 93! I won't do that to my daughter."

According to Carol, her grandmother had done most of the cooking, cleaning, and sewing when she and her sister were youngsters. "Domesticity was never Mother's strong point, perhaps because Granny was always there to take care of things. And Granny was a vigorous woman and mentally sharp until the very end."

For a while after returning to her sunny, airy apartment, Edna felt stronger and seemed to enjoy resuming her activities. Friends called and took her to meetings, which she attended with renewed interest. She and Carol revived their custom of spending a day in Manhattan once a month, visiting museums to see special exhibits, having lunch at a favorite restaurant or trying a new one, sometimes attending a matinee performance of a Broadway play.

But this high did not last long. At home, Edna slipped back into the daily living patterns of her recent past: absentmindedness about meals and medicines, little care about personal hygiene and appearance, and even less care for her apartment, which was a mess unless a cleaning woman had been there recently. Carol engaged a succession of cleaning women before she found a thick-skinned soul who would tolerate the curt, sarcastic remarks that came from Edna in her dark moods.

The apartment was eclectically furnished with pieces from all periods, most scarcely visible under the piles of books and papers scattered everywhere. Numerous framed and unframed photographs on the walls brightened the rooms with pleasant memories. Among the photos were many of Edna, Carol, Bert, and others—frozen at various stages of their lives—on or near sailboats: graceful white hulls and varicolored sails, furled and unfurled.

"Of all the things I've had to give up in the past few years, selling my sloop had to be one of the most painful," Edna sighed. "I miss being able to take her out whenever I want to. Oh, I still go out in their boat with Carol and Bert when they have the time, but it's not the same as sailing my own."

It was Edna who had taught Carol to sail, just as Edna's father had taught her and instilled the love of the sport in her. "My husband was never keen on sailing, so the girls and I went out together in the early days. Later, there were friends who were eager to crew for me. But after that third miserable cataract operation three years ago, I couldn't see worth a damn—so I sold my beautiful little boat. Now I depend on Carol and on the few sailing friends who are still around for an occasional taste of spray."

Edna was so morose, it was plain that she was slipping into a state of depression. More and more, she spoke of how she hated living alone. Carol, despite her mother's avowed opposition to living in their home, talked to Bert about having Edna come to live with them. She speculated that Edna might change her mind if they could convince her that she was welcome.

Bert was uncomfortable with the idea. He was enjoying the privacy and freedom they now had with the two boys out of the house. It was a chance to renew the intimacies of marriage that so often are lost during the middle years. Bert also spoke longingly of his dreams of travel. By arranging for fewer responsibilities at work and at home, now possible for the first time in their married life, he hoped to make those dreams come true. Edna's presence in their home, he felt, was bound to be a deterrent.

Acknowledging that Bert was right, Carol decided to discuss the dilemma with her mother. "You don't want to live with Bert and me, and you don't want to live alone. There must be another way. Got any ideas?"

"What are my choices?" Edna asked, bristling. "I'm not ready for a nursing home yet. On the other hand, I don't think I've got enough energy for Sun City."

"There are all sorts of retirement residences and adult homes," Carol countered.

"Old-age homes, you mean," Edna snorted. Then, more gently: "Look dear, I know you mean well, but why don't we just leave things as they are? After all, at least my misery here is comfortable and familiar."

"I refuse to accept that. And you would, too, if you were your old self. Think of all the community projects you've tackled, all the studies you've done, all the battles you've fought. You have no right to give up now, when it's your own life that's at stake."

Edna sat quietly for a few moments, gazing fondly at her daughter. Finally she said, "Thanks, honey, I needed that. I needed to be reminded that I am a person of worth. When you feel inadequate and useless, you tend to forget all your old strengths. You and I working together should be able to find out what alternatives there are out there and whether any of them fit me."

Once the decision was made to investigate housing options for the elderly, the two women proceeded as though conducting a committee study for one of their organizations. Edna telephoned several area agencies on aging and asked for lists of residences and housing programs. Carol contacted the state housing finance agency and the county community-development department and obtained information on new and proposed projects. They both pored over books and pamphlets from the library.

After the initial research was done, they listed likely alternatives within a 50-mile radius of their home town: specially designed subsidized housing projects, congregate residences, and life-care communities; adult communities (retirement towns and villages) and residential hotels; group-shared homes and board-and-care homes.

They also discussed the possibility of renting the spare bedroom in Edna's apartment to someone who would drive, cook, and assume some of the other household chores as part of a home-sharing arrangement, as well as the possibility of having Edna share another person's home. A county housemate-matching service could help with home-sharing arrangements. Both women also spoke with friends and friends of friends who had changed their living arrangements late in life or who had helped older relatives make such changes.

While all this was going on, Carol—with Edna's consent—made a determined effort to organize the apartment for safety and convenience. She also managed to persuade Edna to attend the daily nutrition program at a nearby church; a van would pick her up at 11

each morning. Previously, Edna had refused to use all such programs, claiming that she had no desire to dine with strangers with
whom she had nothing in common. But Carol argued that having
her main meal of the day at the center would eliminate the need for
cooking and much of the food shopping, that nutritionally sound
meals were important to her health, and that she might be surprised
by the caliber of some of the people who attended. Although she
regularly complained about the food and was critical of the people,
Edna continued to go to the center "to please Carol."

And Carol was pleased. "Edna's a bit of a faker, you know. She
really hates to cook. She's always said, 'Any amount of domesticity
is too much for me.' Now she doesn't have to fuss around in the
kitchen any more. And I don't have to worry about her setting the
place on fire. Plus, the kitchen, which always used to be a mess,
stays fairly clean now. On Sunday, she usually has dinner at my
house. On Saturday, she improvises. But the main thing is that she's
being fairly well fed." Carol also reported that Edna had joined an
afternoon bridge group at the center.

Late afternoons and nights were still long and lonely, however.
Formerly an avid reader, Edna felt frustrated and unhappy at the
difficulties caused by her poor vision; even with the strong lenses she
wore, she often had to use a magnifying glass. Large-type books and
audiotapes helped somewhat, but many of the titles were of limited
appeal to her. "What I miss most are the lively discussions, the arguments, the sense of challenge and involvement of the old days,"
she explained, adding, "I hate talking to myself!"

Asked again whether she might reconsider and move into Carol's
home, at least until she found a more suitable living arrangement,
Edna answered, "God, no! I had my mother living with me all those
years. It's so important to have your own place, so important for
both of us to have our privacy. The trick is to have privacy when
you want it and companionship when you want it. In a good marriage, you achieve a balance, as I think I did. And until I quit driving, I could always go out and seek companionship. Now," she
shrugged, "I'm no longer in control. I seem to have to take things as
they come. There must be a better way for me to live—and I hope
Carol and I can find it."

Essentially, Edna's and Carol's search is our search—the reason for this book. What follows should help other women and men in similar situations, at a crossroad in life where unfamiliar trails lead to unknown destinations. In mapping out this territory, we describe traditional housing for the elderly, as well as innovative concepts in shared and cooperative living taking shape throughout the country. And at the end, we return to Edna and Carol and complete their story.

# 2

# Come, Let Us Live Together!

*Group-shared homes*

"WHY should my mom want to go and live with a group of strangers?" That's the first question you might ask if a shared group home were suggested as a solution to your mother's housing needs.

There is no simple answer. Much depends on her personality, her health, her finances, her present housing situation, and her family's attitudes (and that includes you). Before a decision can be made, of course, you and your mother will want to know a good deal more about shared living: what it means, who practices it, and how successful it is.

When at least 5 to as many as 15 unrelated people agree to live together and share the expenses and some or all of the work of maintaining a household, a *shared group home* is formed.

Does this sound vaguely familiar, like the communes we or our children might have joined in the 1960s? That's because the basic idea is the same: people banding together to satisfy certain economic and social needs. Communes were attempts to reap the economic and energy-saving benefits of cooperative living and to create a sense of family as an anchor during chaotic times.

Older people are now banding together for many of the same reasons—for economy, companionship, and support. The major difference is that community assistance is often required for the creation and continued existence of many of these "elder communes."

Ideally, a group of friends could buy and renovate or build a house for shared living in their later years. Perhaps there are some such households, and there certainly should be more in the future. To do it yourself, however, requires the kind of will, energy, and physical stamina that may be in short supply when you are older. It is best to start before it is too late.

Fortunately, growing awareness of housing needs by people of all ages has sparked interest and action in this field, and more and more shared group homes are being sponsored and operated by such community organizations as churches, civic associations, advocacy groups, and government agencies. Ownership of these homes is usually vested in a nonprofit corporation formed by the sponsor or a coalition of sponsors. There are also for-profit owners; Share-a-Home in Florida is one of the earliest examples. Joint ownership by tenants and single resident-owners who rent to the other house residents are less common.

The benefits of community involvement and nonprofit sponsorship during the process of finding and establishing a shared group home are manifold. Volunteers with financial, legal, and real-estate expertise can help keep preliminary costs down; those who can help with plumbing, carpentry, electrical work, decorating, and the like during renovation of the house (usually, but not always, a large old house) are equally valuable. The more people who pitch in the better, not just for reasons of economy, but because they will become champions of the house, thus assuring greater acceptance by the rest of the community. And once the house is occupied, the sponsor may need to tap community resources for any social and economic support needed by the residents.

After they are set up, some group-sharing homes for the elderly function with little outside assistance; the residents themselves manage the cooking, shopping, cleaning, and light maintenance. At the other extreme are the homes that have live-in full-time housekeepers or managers. In between are shared homes with varying degrees of staff or volunteer help for meal planning and preparation, household chores, and social needs. The amount of assistance required usually depends on the physical capabilities of the residents. For the most part, shared living arrangements are set up with the emphasis on the most self-reliance possible.

The growing elderly population and the scarcity of affordable housing in many communities has prompted a surge of interest in shared group homes throughout the country, although the numbers in operation are still small. Before interest can be converted into actuality, however, there are many obstacles to overcome. Is the result worth all the planning, labor, and education? The best way to find out is to meet some of the "strangers" who live together in a few of these sharing houses and some of their sponsors and boosters.

Our first visit was to Parkside, a large, three-story house built in the 1930s in a medium-sized town in a middle Atlantic state. The house stood comfortably on a side street with other large houses of that era and a few smaller, newer ones. Old trees cast pleasant shadows, and a small town park occupying the corner lot to the right was cool and inviting, its greenery partially shielding the house from the traffic on the main street. It was a sunny day in late spring, and we could hear the voices of children playing in the park as we and our friend Peggy left her car at the curb in front of Parkside. Peggy's mother, Jean, waited on the front porch. She waved and called out a greeting as we walked down the path skirting the lawn. Peggy introduced us to her mother and to Virginia, who were waiting together on the porch. "Virginia is one of the family here," Jean told us. Both the older women proudly showed us through the house.

The house had been remodeled to accommodate seven older adults. At the time, five women and two men lived there. Each had a private bedroom and shared a bathroom with one other person. The common rooms were all on the first floor.

Entering, we were in a hallway with a small sitting area on the right, near a window. The enclosed staircase to the upper floors started here. A room to the left, probably the original parlor, belonged to Belle. She said she chose the downstairs room because arthritis in her legs made climbing stairs difficult. The others said privately that Belle chose the room because "she's too fat" and because "she's nosy and likes being near the door." So Belle became the unofficial doorkeeper.

The living room at the end of the hallway was a large square, furnished with a flowery, chintz-covered couch, two well-stuffed armchairs, a large television set, and one darkly polished Queen Anne table. Virginia remarked that the table and the large, ornate lamp on it came from her home. Belle, who had joined us, said that she contributed the couch and coffee table. A few other furnishings were brought in by residents; the rest were donated or bought with funds donated by the sponsoring church's congregation and by the community. All the bedrooms were furnished with their owners' personal possessions.

No one turned on the television set the afternoon we were there. Because of our visit? Jean said, "No. We don't usually turn it on until after dinner, unless there's something special, like a parade or World Series game. A few of us watch soap operas and a couple of morning shows, but we've all got our own small TVs in our rooms."

Half of the wall at the far end of the living room was open to a large dining room. The kitchen, with a pass-through counter and wide entry to the dining room, occupied the rest of the space behind the living room. The completely modernized kitchen was sparkling clean. A calendar tacked to the wall listed two names for each day, a schedule of kitchen helpers for the housekeeper, Mrs. R——, who prepared seven dinner meals per week. Except for Sunday afternoon when the residents reheated and served the meal themselves, Mrs. R—— and her two assistants-of-the-day served the evening meal.

The housekeeper, a middle-aged divorcee and former school cafeteria cook, lived in a small apartment on the third floor. She cleaned the common rooms and bathrooms and changed and washed linens once each week; she also did all the marketing, kept records of expenditures, mediated arguments among the residents, and took charge in emergencies.

Residents were responsible for preparing their own breakfasts and lunches and for cleaning their rooms. If someone was ill, one of the other residents fixed a tray.

"Three of us—Virginia, Belle, and I—almost always have breakfast together. And lunch, too, if we're not out somewhere. Sometimes one of the others joins us. Jim is up very early and usually eats breakfast alone. He likes to work outdoors when the weather is good, and he does custodial work at the church around the corner three mornings a week. Christa sometimes comes down to eat with him," Jean explained.

A compact, chunky woman with light hazel eyes and streaks of black in her gray hair, Jean moved about energetically and seemed in good health. "To look at her you wouldn't think she'd had two serious heart attacks," our friend Peggy said.

Peggy had described her mother's background during the drive to Parkside. Widowed at age 38, Jean had trained as a hospital lab technician in the city where she and her husband, an accountant, had lived in a spacious, three-bedroom apartment in a good residential neighborhood. After completing her training, Jean was employed by a large metropolitan hospital, a job she kept for 30 years until forced to retire at age 70. During all those years, she lived alone in the same apartment, traveling to her job by bus and subway.

She expected to live there for the rest of her life, according to Peggy. "The trouble was that the old neighborhood, which was so nice when my older brother and I were growing up, was changing for the worse. Then came Mom's first heart attack. Fortunately, she had enough time and presence of mind to get to the phone and call for help. Otherwise . . . " Peggy shuddered.

After years as a broker working for others, Peggy had recently opened her own real-estate office. Attractive and blond, she resembled her mother only in her tendency to plumpness and her ready smile. But their affection and concern for each other was obvious. All Jean's conversations were sprinkled with remarks about how good and how bright her daughter always had been.

While Jean lived in the city, she had been separated from her daughter by a distance of over 100 miles, keeping in touch by phone two or three times a week. Jean, who never learned to drive, would ride a train out to see Peggy and her family once every few months. She visited her son and his family in Texas twice a year. Any other free time was spent with numerous friends. But as the years advanced, many old friends moved away or died. The few who remained met daily at the local senior center, but all were fearful of being out after dark, of using elevators, even of shopping in some of the stores that had replaced the old, familiar ones.

"There were so many muggings you had to screw up your courage to enter a building or an elevator alone, day or night. I began to feel like a prisoner in my own apartment, especially in wintertime," Jean remembered. "Shopping and cleaning got to be a big deal, too. It seemed to be taking all my energy just to keep alive."

After her second heart attack, Jean consented to using household help. "It was hard to get used to an outsider puttering around with things I'd taken care of by myself all my life. And it wasn't easy to find someone I could trust. Usually they were single women with family responsibilities, and they didn't always show up."

At Peggy's insistence, her mother began spending longer periods

of time at Peggy's home; in the last few years before moving to Parkside, Jean had stayed over the three summer months. "When she
went back to the city, I constantly worried about her," Peggy said.
"We pleaded with her to give up the apartment and move in with us,
but she refused. Much as she loved her grandchildren, she said, bed-
lam was too mild a word to describe our house when they were
there. And they were home for much of the summer—piling in with
friends, partying, playing their noisy music. Three teenagers can be
wearing on anybody's nerves, let alone an older person who's used
to living quietly by herself."

Even when the three children had gone off to college, Peggy and
her husband (a high-school teacher) could not persuade her mother
to move to their house. "Everyone needs their privacy, their own
space," Jean had insisted.

For Peggy, her mother's refusal meant long, exhausting drives
into the city to reassure herself about Jean's safety or to pick her up
for a "country visit." At the same time, Peggy's new real-estate office
demanded a great deal of attention, and such family crises as a series
of diagnostic tests and surgery for her husband, a son's dropping out
of college, and her daughter's ending an unhappy love affair all added
to the strain.

During this period, Peggy searched for a small house or apartment in town for her mother. But such housing seemed prohibitively
expensive compared with Jean's rent-controlled apartment in the
city. Jean's income was limited to Social Security and a small union
pension, her savings had been depleted by long hospital stays and
follow-up care, and she was fiercely determined to pay her own
way—all of which ruled out costly housing alternatives.

"The best hope seemed to be our church committee to help the
elderly. When I joined, I was amazed at how many people in the
congregation were in a similar fix, with aging parents living alone,
some of them far away—in Florida or California or Arizona—and
ailing." Peggy described how the committee investigated various
housing options, gathering information about other community efforts and inviting speakers to describe their experiences and the results of their endeavors. It soon became apparent that the most practical project the church committee could work on would be a small
group-sharing home.

"The concept was appealing, too," Peggy commented. "It seemed like an economical, dignified, caring atmosphere for older people like my mom who shouldn't or didn't want to live alone or with their kids. It turned out to be a lot of work by a lot of people for only a handful of residents. But I really think it was worth it."

Peggy worked with the property committee and was instrumental in finding the house and shepherding the sale through to closing. "From then on I took a back seat. And that was okay, because word about the project had spread by then, and more people had joined us. That's about the time you got involved, Virginia," Peggy said, turning to her mother's friend.

Virginia laughed. "What a time we had! What hassles! So many permits, licenses, approvals, and what-alls to get. And all from different agencies of the town, county, and state. Seemed like there were hundreds of them."

Virginia—thin, wiry, and girlish despite her white hair—had a room on the third floor. She seemed to run up and down stairs at will. At 72, she was the youngest resident of Parkside. Continuing her description of the planning and work that went into the remodeling of the house, she spoke of how the architect worked with the property committee to ascertain the changes needed, then drew up blueprints without charging a fee. The housing corporation formed to develop and manage Parkside, serving as general contractor, delegated the church building committee to obtain bids, enter into contracts, and check on the progress of the work.

"You wouldn't believe how much pleading and praying and even shouting was involved. Teams of us would show up every day to push the construction along," Virginia exclaimed. "That and cleaning up were the hard parts. The fun part was the interior painting and decorating. It was all done by volunteers with a little help and advice from a couple of professionals. Everyone pitched in. My son and two little grandsons spent a couple of weekends here wielding paintbrushes. I think Peggy's daughter helped out a few times, and Belle's grandchildren, too."

Oddly, Virginia never considered living at Parkside while working on the project. She and her husband lived about a mile away from Parkside in a pleasant cottage that was their home for almost all of the 48 years of their marriage. A few months after Parkside opened, he died suddenly of a cerebral hemorrhage. "I felt as if the ground fell away. I never felt so alone in my life. I was terrified at night. Every sound was magnified. I would listen to my heart beating and imagine that it had stopped," Virginia remembered sadly.

It was Virginia's son who suggested that she try living at Parkside. He arranged for her house to be rented, assuring her that if she changed her mind she could come back to it. "I've been living here about eight months. Now my renters, who have a one-year lease with an option to buy, say they want to buy the house. I don't think I want to go back, but I have a few months to make up my mind. One thing is sure," Virginia added, "I don't want to leave this town, and this location is wonderful. My church is just around the corner, and I like being close enough to walk to the library, bank, and stores that I'm used to. I'm nervous about driving, and I only do it when I absolutely must."

Virginia still does volunteer work with the churchwomen's group and has added baby-sitting for neighbors to her activities since coming to live at Parkside. Earning a little money was a new experience for her as she had never held a job outside of her home, and she enjoyed being with children. All told, she seemed to like her life at Parkside. "Of course, I don't have the privacy I had in my own home. On the other hand, I never feel as lonely or frightened as I did when I was alone."

Talking with the residents' committee chairwoman gave us further insight into the nature of this particular shared home and of its tenants. Mabel P——, a social worker in her early 40s, served as counselor and administrator of Parkside on a voluntary basis. She spent several hours each week at the house checking into any problems the housekeeper or residents might have, reported on the status of the house to the full church committee, and was on call at all times.

"There are always disappointments and frustrations when you work with a group of individuals in a sharing situation like this," Mabel noted. "But in this case, the pluses so far outweigh the minuses, there's no doubt at all about its tremendous value.

"Here you have frail old people who were feeling very shaky about their lives when they were alone out there. Put them together and they gain strength, enough to cope, anyway, and to keep them from being a burden to their children and out of nursing homes—the two things they dread most."

Mabel's forceful, clipped manner seemed at odds with the compassion in her words as she spoke about the residents and what brought them to Parkside. One of the residents, Jim, had tried to drown himself the year before. After devotedly caring for his wife, who was ill with cancer for many years, he became profoundly depressed when she died. Unable to stay in his apartment alone, he was shunted between his two sons' homes for three months at a time. "I thought I'd go nuts," he said in his slurred speech, one of the results of a head wound he received while in the army during World War II.

After Jim's suicide attempt, he was placed in the psychiatric ward of a Veterans Administration hospital and treated for depression. "There was no question about the diagnosis. He missed nursing his wife and having a home. Apparently, one son's wife was very resentful of his presence in her home. He felt unwanted, unneeded, unloved—yet trapped by his dependence. Suicide is not that unusual among old people. I read somewhere that one out of five suicides is a person who is 65 or older," Mabel said.

Jim's son, who owned a furniture store in town, heard a church committee member speak on the group home at a Chamber of Commerce meeting. Jim was about to be released from the hospital, and his doctor had strongly recommended a more permanent and less emotion-fraught living arrangement than the previous one. The son and father visited Parkside, liked what they saw, and filled out the application forms. The next step was an informal interview with two residents' committee members to establish that Jim genuinely wanted to live at Parkside and that his family concurred.

Mabel, who was one of the interviewers, remembered how touched she was by Jim's eagerness to please. "He's a shy man, so it wasn't easy for him to speak, and he let his son do most of the talking. But once in a while he would interject a comment like 'I'm very handy at fixing things,' or, 'I can take care of the garden and mow the lawn.' All of which proved to be true. And in the year and a half he's been here, he's also relaxed a little in his relationships with the others. He's not nearly as reclusive. And he's especially kind to Christa, our oldest resident."

Jim, at 76, was still muscular. Tall, with sparse, sandy-gray hair, he walked with his eyes downcast and a shambling gait. When we were introduced, a fleeting smile crossed his face when he looked up. Asked how he felt about living at Parkside, Jim replied, "It took some getting used to, but now I like it fine. I'm my own man here for the first time in a long time."

Christa, who was 88, small, shriveled, and with skin like fine parchment, came to Parkside from a nursing home. Her own apartment had been a shambles—neglected, cluttered, dirty—and her son had refused to let her return there after a hospital stay. She had fallen in the bathroom and had lain on the tile floor with a broken shoulder and arm and two cracked ribs until discovered by a neighbor nearly two days later.

An active, restless person, Christa continually demanded her removal from the nursing home. A staff social worker, who had learned about Parkside at a seminar on housing for the elderly, suggested it as a possible alternative. Christa's son and his wife investigated, then took Christa to the house. "I wasn't wild about the idea of living with a bunch of strangers. I would infinitely have preferred going back to my own place. Given my limited choices, however, I could see that this would be a vast improvement over the nursing home," Christa said, summing up her reaction.

Widowed 20 years earlier, Christa had worked as an assistant principal at a large city high school. Soon after her retirement, she recruited a woman friend to join her on a year's tour around the United States in a large camper. After the trip, she lived in New Mexico with an old college friend, a man she met again while traveling, until the relationship soured and she headed east again. An apartment in the city in which she had worked was her last home. She spoke excitedly about all the concerts she had heard and plays she had seen. "Now I can barely hear anything," she moaned. "I don't miss much here, but I would like to hear music well played and reverberating in a great hall once again."

Mabel's evaluation of Christa emphasized her spunkiness. With only a cane, Christa made her way to the library, post office, and stores by herself, sometimes walking long distances. As for the hearing impairment, Mabel said, "It's genuine, but she does have a hearing aid. However, I believe she uses it selectively. She doesn't like chatting with the other women, although she's polite enough. When

Jim talks, that's another story. She watches his lips very carefully, and he looks at her and speaks very distinctly. They have a special relationship—like mother and son."

Christa's only child, her son, lived about 50 miles north of Parkside. He and his wife were very attentive when they came to visit; occasionally they would take Christa out for the day, more rarely to their home for the weekend. Otherwise, Jim looked after her, helping her up the stairs to her second-floor room or making her a cup of tea when she appeared, bleary-eyed from lack of sleep, in the kitchen at dawn.

Had she ever considered living with her son? "Never!" Christa answered vehemently. "It's a catastrophe to lose your own home. But to impose yourself on someone else's life and deprive him of privacy, especially your own child, because of ties of birth, is unforgivable. I'll do well enough here until it's time to go. At least on the nights I can't sleep, I can come down to the kitchen and make myself a cup of tea."

Belle and Jean were the first residents in the house. Christa and Jim followed a few months later, and after them came an 89-year-old woman who stayed only a few months before she had to be moved to a nursing home because of various medical problems. Not until the end of the first year had Virginia moved in, and Rose and Bill came soon after. Thus, it took about a year for the house to be completely occupied. This caused a drain on finances, as the resident's fee of $475 per month had been calculated to keep Parkside self-sustaining on the basis of full occupancy.

"The problem," Mabel explained, "was not just getting the news out. The church public-relations committee did a great job. They contacted all the area churches, hospitals, and social agencies. They sent press releases and paid ads to the newspapers. We held two open houses. The difficulty was getting people to accept the idea of shared living."

Did she feel the living arrangement was beneficial to all the current residents? "Without exception," Mabel answered. "Take Belle. When she first came, she was very lethargic. She sat in her room all day watching TV. Her daughter Judy came to check on her every day—to see that she took her medicine and to pick up her personal laundry or bring her little things she might need, tissues and such. Judy worried because her mother had behaved the same way during the two years she'd lived at Judy's house. In fact, this unwillingness to care for herself after her husband's death forced Belle to give up her own home. Her arthritis is bad, of course. But even with medication to control it, she had given up completely.

"Now," Mabel continued, "she often joins the others for meetings and luncheons at the church or on short shopping trips. And she's taken on more responsibility for herself. Not long ago, she actually scolded Judy for coming every day. This indicates to me that Belle has finally let go of her resentment at being 'put out' of Judy's home."

Weekly meetings with the residents help Mabel assess their adjustment to living at Parkside. She also meets with family members at their request, or hers, whenever problems arise. The time period for "settling in" varied, but Mabel felt that in general, all the current residents had made a good adjustment.

Jean had adjusted fairly quickly, possibly because of Peggy's involvement and because of the agreement between mother and daughter that once the house was finished, Jean would move in. So they both had a long time to get used to the idea.

Belle took longer to accept her new home. But soon after Virginia came to live there, Belle began to snap out of her lethargy. According to Mabel, "Virginia's energy seems to be contagious. She's truly a valuable resource here. If she could overcome her fear of being alone, she could probably return to her old home and manage quite well for many years. But I don't believe she will go back. I think she feels more useful here and more in command of her life than she has since her children were little."

Jim and Christa had reached a state of equilibrium almost immediately; both having come from institutional settings, they were keenly aware of the improvement in their status. But because Christa was so frail, Mabel was not certain how long she could continue to live there.

The newest residents, Bill and Rose, had been at Parkside for only a few months. Bill had just turned 80. A heavy, barrel-chested man with a ruddy complexion, he had been a florist until a few years earlier. His wife had been dead for 15 years, but Bill had stayed in their large apartment in a suburb close to the city where his flower shop was located. Later, suffering from hypertension and diabetes, he sold the shop and the apartment and moved into a boarding house. Every few months he drove out to visit his granddaughter and her family, his closest relatives; his son had died in the Korean War. On the last of these trips, he fell asleep at the wheel and smashed his car into a concrete embankment.

After his release from the hospital, Bill returned to the boarding house. His granddaughter offered him a room in her small house at least until his broken legs mended and he was mobile again. " 'No thanks, Honey,' I told her. She's got a job and four little kids to look after, bless 'em. 'But,' I said, 'If you can find me a nice place near you, I'd like that a lot.' And this is the place she found for me. Smart girl!" Bill smiled and waved his cane in a circle to indicate the house and all it held for him, including the flower beds and borders, now showing their bright blossoms; he had planted and tended them this season, his first at Parkside.

It was difficult to determine from talking with Rose whether or not she liked living at Parkside. She was friendly but perplexed, saying she could not remember exactly how she came to live there. She did know that one son and a daughter lived nearby, that they had helped her make the move, and that she saw them and their families quite often. Once a beautiful woman, 81-year-old Rose had poor vision, applied her cosmetics liberally, wore elaborate outfits, and scented the air with her perfumes and colognes.

"The others tend to ignore her because her memory is so bad and she tells the same stories over and over again. But they do remind her of special dates and activities, and they take her with them to church and shopping. She was pretty wilted when she came—quite confused. But it didn't take long before she perked up," said Mabel.

"These people aren't really a family; they have no common history or permanent ties to bind them together," Mabel continued. "And if they let themselves think about it, the impermanence can be downright scary. In spite of this, some of them become friends. And they all know they can count on one another. And for back-up they have a younger—and more permanent—relative nearby.

"The need for companionship, security, and housekeeping help at a reasonable cost is what brought them here. I believe they've found them. And they know they can stay for as long as their health and strength hold out. Best of all, they know they can have as much independence as they can handle without the loneliness and insecurity of living alone or the guilty feeling of burdening their children," Mabel observed.

The five elderly residents of Grove Cottage, hundreds of miles away in a small town bordering a large metropolitan area in the Midwest, were motivated by similar needs. The house was situated at the eastern end of a four-block shopping strip on the main street, which bisects the town and meets the old highway at both ends. The rest of the town is residential, a bedroom community. A half-acre grove of tall pine trees behind Grove Cottage accounts for its name.

The wood siding on the two-story house was neatly painted a light tan color; the shutters were brown. The small front lawn was bright with pansies and begonias; there were narrow side yards and a large back yard with rustic wood chairs and a large rectangular plank table under a spreading maple tree. A small garden plot on one side was planted with tomatoes, peppers, squash, and other summer vegetables. A short, thin, sinewy man was weeding the garden with a long-handled hoe. His name was George; he was 77 years old and had lived at Grove Cottage since it opened two years earlier.

The creation of Grove Cottage began when the house, gutted by fire, was given to the church across the road. A coalition of area churches raised the money to rebuild the 100-year-old structure. The town gave its full sanction and cooperation, and church congregations and the community as a whole were generous with labor and material donations. The entire process took eight months.

As with Parkside, it took nearly a year to fill the five bedrooms— four upstairs with two baths and one on the main floor at the back of the house. Living room, kitchen, and dining room were shared. The basement, used mainly for storage, had a small workshop area. This was especially important to George, who was a carpenter.

George had been the town's carpenter for as long as most people could remember. Conscientious, capable, and trustworthy were words people used to describe George and his work. All the old-timers knew the story of how George's young bride had come down with polio and how he took care of her for more than 40 years. Then George himself fell ill; he had a serious heart attack and had to undergo double bypass surgery and stay in the hospital for six weeks. The minister and a committee of churchwomen arranged to move his invalid wife to a nursing home.

George would have taken her home again after his release, but the doctors advised against it. By that time, too, his meager savings had been spent on hospital and nursing-care bills. Neither he nor his wife had any known relatives. George's parents, who had worked a farm about three miles from the town center on land that now sprouted houses, and his older brother, who had run off to Alaska in his teens, were long gone. George thought he had nowhere to go but back to the small apartment behind his carpentry shop just off Main Street, until the minister suggested he consider moving to Grove Cottage and serving as caretaker.

The rebuilt house was almost ready for occupancy by the time George left the hospital. The Cottage Coalition had agreed that residents would have to be at least 62 years old, ambulatory, able to attend to their own personal needs, and willing to abide by a few minimal rules. They would furnish and care for their own rooms, cooperate with each other when using the common rooms, and pay a monthly charge that would cover the cost of house maintenance, food, housekeeping, utilities, and other household expenses. A rental agreement was drawn up, and the monthly charge was set at $400.

"We tried to keep the monthly rental low by providing only those services that were absolutely necessary," said Betty K——, the coalition's director. "The original concept was to give the group as much responsibility and autonomy as possible. Our hope was that the residents would pull together and behave as a family. And in many ways they do, right down to the squabbling and bickering," she laughed.

A housekeeper cleaned the common rooms, did all the food shopping, and cooked and served five main meals per week. Otherwise the residents were on their own. A list of emergency numbers was posted next to the phone, but there was no outsider to take charge. "Well, we soon learned that an authority figure is needed," Betty remarked. "And we were fortunate to have George here from the beginning. Not that he's bossy. But he does act as mediator when disagreements come up, and he calls me if he can't settle them. He's also the caretaker: checking the doors and the lights at night, watching out for needed repairs, taking charge in an emergency."

George's room on the second floor overlooked the back yard and one side of the house. (Each of the bedrooms was at a corner of the house and had two windows, one on each right-angle exterior wall.) Roughspun blue drapes hung at the windows. His own sturdy, handmade wood furniture of good, simple design stood against the walls. The 14-foot-square room was as neat as an army barracks waiting for inspection.

Paula's room, across the landing, was more cluttered and colorful: photographs everywhere, bright needlework designs on cushions, a hooked rug on top of the neutral beige carpeting that was found throughout the house (as a safety measure), lacy, white curtains on the windows.

Paula was an exuberant 85, as talkative as George was silent. She had lived at Grove Cottage for almost a year but still owned the house in the next town in which she had lived for more than a half century. Her husband was born in that same house, and now her newly married grandson lived there.

Couldn't Paula have stayed and shared the house with the newlyweds? Why had she come to live at Grove Cottage instead?

"It's complicated," Paula answered. "I have five children, twelve grandchildren, and a couple of great-grandchildren. And at one time or another, one or more of them have come to live with me. Not for long, though. They always move on, back to their own lives.

"A few years ago, when I was very ill—first with flu and then pneumonia—my oldest daughter came to stay with me. But she was anxious to get back to her job and her husband, so she hired a housekeeper companion for me. It was an expensive arrangement, so when I felt a little better, I let her go and tried to manage with a part-time maid." Here Paula launched into a hilarious account of her experiences with a succession of "moppets and misfits" who often "relied more on me than I ever dared rely on them.

"It was very tiring," she sighed. "And I realized that the house itself had become a terrible burden in the eight years since my husband had died. Things breaking down every other day, sometimes twice a day. Yard work and painting had to be done. Bills to pay. I felt so alone. Friends died and moved away. I became so nervous and depressed, I stopped driving and never went anywhere."

When Paula complained to her children, they advised her to sell the house, and two of her daughters invited her to come and live with them. "Except for getting the weight of the house off my shoulders, I couldn't figure how that would be an improvement," Paula reflected. "They're out all day, and I'd be just as lonely as ever. And in a strange place, to boot!"

It was Paula's favorite grandson, Neil, who discovered Grove Cottage. Stopping in town on one of his occasional visits, he stood watching the painters put the finishing touches on the house. A tall man in clerical clothing stood beside him, looking up with a pleased smile at the two workmen on their ladders. Neil wondered whether there might be more work to do on the house. He was handy, he said, and he could use the money. The minister laughed, saying that very little money was being paid for work on that particular house. As it turned out, Neil volunteered to do some interior painting. And he brought his grandmother to see the house.

"The house looked nice enough, but the idea of sharing it with other people—people who aren't family—sounded awful. Neil kept telling me how much fun he'd had sharing a big, old, tumbledown farmhouse while he was at college. I kept thinking that when you're young, anything goes," Paula remembered.

Neil did not let the matter lie, however. He promoted the idea among his parents, aunts, and uncles. Each of them who visited that year went to look at Grove Cottage and talk with someone from the coalition. By the end of the following winter, Paula had agreed to try living at Grove Cottage on condition that she could return to her house if she did not like group living. She was assured that all prospective tenants were encouraged to keep their former homes for at least a month while trying the new arrangement.

"It took awhile to get used to, and I was tempted to leave a couple of times at the beginning. But now if I think of going back, it's like thinking of going into solitary confinement," Paula mused. "I just hope I can keep my wits and my works in order, so I don't have to move on," she added, referring to two of the former residents who had to be moved into nursing homes.

"Oh Paula, don't talk like that. You're the one who takes care of the rest of us," a voice piped up. It was Sally, who had come out to the back yard to sit with us. Her daughter-in-law, Mavis, a plump woman in her early 40s was with her. They had just returned from the county hospital, where Sally attended a physiotherapy session twice a week.

Sally, the youngest of the Grove Cottage residents, was 66, of medium height and weight, and had a pleasant face and soft, gray eyes. A stroke resulted in paralysis of her right side, but she had made a good recovery in the intervening three years. She walked slowly, using a cane, but with only a slight drag of her right foot. Her right arm appeared normal, but the hand lacked dexterity. Her speech was slow and deliberate. Widowed ten years before, she had continued to live in the small house she and her husband, a merchant seaman, had bought in their middle age.

"We'd always lived in rentals in different port cities around the country," Sally reminisced. "So when we bought that little house near the Gulf, it meant an awful lot to us. And when my husband died, I couldn't bring myself to leave it. Besides, I was used to being alone—he was away at sea so much of the time."

After her stroke, Sally was in no condition to maintain her own home. Bob, her only child, sold her house and took her north to live in his home, a few miles from Grove Cottage. There, Bob, Mavis, and their three children showered Sally with love and attention. Under their care and with professional rehabilitation therapy, she improved steadily.

Sally spoke glowingly of her family. "They treated me like a queen. Anything I wanted, they got for me. I can't tell you how kind and thoughtful they all were—and still are. Of course, I loved being fussed over. But after a while, I wanted to help out a little, to pull my own weight around the house."

Mavis had given Sally small tasks, such as cooking, mending, and sweeping the front walk. But as she grew stronger, Sally grew more restless. "It's a small house, and I kept feeling as if I were in the way. I had taken my grandson's room—he slept on an old couch in the basement. And I'd been there almost two years, being waited on hand and foot. Finally, I told Bob and Mavis I thought I ought to move out to an apartment or a boarding hotel, if there were any nearby."

Mavis continued with the story: "We were really shocked. We all thought she was doing so well and that she was happy living with us. It seemed like maybe we were at fault."

Once recovered from her surprise but still feeling guilty, Mavis talked to her parson, then to her husband, about Grove Cottage. Bob's immediate reaction was rejection. "I'm not going to put my mom into an old-folks' home."

Mavis had repeated the parson's arguments: "It's a different kind of home. The people who live there will be like a family. They'll look after each other. Each one has a bedroom, and they all share the rest of the house. It sounds good to me. You know George, the carpenter? Well, he just moved in. The church committee is paying him a small amount to be caretaker. That'll help him pay his rent."

Bob, who was an electrician, knew George well as they had worked on construction jobs together. And he respected George as a man and a craftsman. He knew that George had sold his shop living quarters to the local hardware merchant who wanted to expand his store and that the money had been used to pay medical and nursing-care bills. And he was impressed that George had chosen to live at Grove Cottage. After mulling it over for a while, Bob stopped in to talk to George and to look the place over. He approved of what he saw.

Sally's first impressions were of spaciousness and serenity, both in sharp contrast to her family's home. She was delighted that the stores, post office, library, and bus stop were all just down the street, which meant she need not rely on her family to drive her everywhere. "It was a relief to be on my own again. Although . . . I did miss the kids for a while after I left—the liveliness, even the arguments. But I see them all so often. And I enjoy being with them more now that I know I can leave at the end of the day and come back here to my other family—the quiet one."

The rest of the cottage family, Carl and Louise, had joined us in the yard to catch the late afternoon breezes of a warm summer day. Carl, a thin, faded-looking man in his late 80s wearing a crumpled linen sport coat and a tie despite the heat, used his cane in the manner of a blind man, though he still had some dim vision. He also wore a hearing aid and, nodding very politely when spoken to, seemed to understand.

Carl had come to live at Grove Cottage by sheer chance. When he could no longer manage in his own home because of his failing vision, his two daughters began investigating nursing homes. A doctor at one of these homes, after examining Carl and finding him in good health except for his failing eyesight and hearing loss, told his daughters about the shared group home.

"My youngest girl brought me out here to look the place over," Carl related in a quavery voice. "I wasn't too keen on coming. I'd much rather have stayed in my house, but the girls kept worrying I'd burn the place down. Anyway, it seemed a lot better than a nursing home, so I said I'd try it for a while. Now I wish I'd come years ago, instead of living alone so long."

Carl had been a dentist in the central city, married to a grade-school teacher who died about 20 years earlier. He was to have married again a few years after being widowed, but his fiancee became ill and died. "After that I gave up on romance," he said with a trace of a smile.

"Nonsense!" boomed Paula. "There's probably a gal out there right now—just waiting for you."

Louise, the fifth member of the household, chuckled. A sturdy, matronly looking woman, tall and vigorous for her 73 years, she had been a bank teller and then an assistant bank manager until her retirement 11 years earlier. She had never married and had no intention of ever leaving her apartment in the city, where she enjoyed attending sports and cultural events.

In later years, Louise shared her apartment with a younger sister who had been widowed. Because Louise suffered several minor heart attacks after a lifetime of good health, she found the companionship comforting. When her sister died of a massive heart attack, she felt frightened and alone and began a search for another companion. Her niece, the dead sister's daughter, then suggested that she move to Grove Cottage, which was near the niece's home. Although resistant at first, Louise agreed to a trial residence. Three months later, she notified her city landlord that she was giving up the apartment— after 45 years.

"That was last month. And it was a wrench, believe me," Louise said primly. "But my doctor tells me my health has improved. This good country air, don't y'know." She added that she still used her old doctor in the city. The bus that stopped in front of the post office took her to the railroad station, where she could board a citybound train. Total traveling time one way was one and one-half hours, but

Louise said she enjoyed the trip and traveled to the city at least once each week to see friends.

While we talked, George came out with a pitcher of ice tea and some glasses. He had just returned from a visit with his wife. No matter what the weather, as long as the bus ran George made the trip to the nursing home three or four times a week.

In the kitchen, the housekeeper was starting preparations for dinner. After drinking their tea, Louise and Sally went inside to help. Paula and Carl chatted about the luncheon meeting they had been to that day at the church across the road. George stood nearby with a hose, watering the vegetable garden. The pleasant sounds of pots and dishes and women's voices came through the open windows.

Soon Betty, the volunteer director, found us. It was time to leave. As we said our goodbyes, Paula took Carl's arm, and they walked slowly and carefully toward the back door. George was coiling up the hose. The good smells of cooking food wafted out to us. Except for their ages, this might have been any family getting ready for dinner.

A confirmed city dweller might have a difficult time adapting to a shared group home in a suburban or small-town setting. Nevertheless, it can be done. Jean accepted living at Parkside in order to be near her daughter Peggy; Louise settled at Grove Cottage, after all her years of city living, to be near her niece. Proximity to a caring relative is a significant factor in any decision about where an elderly person ought to relocate.

If you are wondering whether there are any small urban group homes for an elderly relative who is attached to city living, the answer is yes, but not many. Small communal households have been set up in several cities. The one we visited, which we call Valdene, is in a high-rise apartment building in a middle-class neighborhood in a northeastern city.

Valdene consists of a cluster of five three-bedroom apartments in a 22-story building. The apartments are rented and supervised by a community service agency. With the permission of the landlord, the kitchen, dining-room, and living-room walls between two adjacent apartments were removed to create large communal areas for serving the main meal every day and for resident meetings and parties.

A resident manager, who lives in a separate apartment in the building, does all the marketing and cooking with the help of two part-time assistants; she also supervises the cleaning staff and is on around-the-clock call. A social worker/counselor spends 15 hours each week with the residents, discussing problems ranging from personality clashes between apartment mates to general complaints from the group. When a resident moves in, she may need special help to overcome feelings of rejection and insecurity.

Valdene was conceived as an answer to a long nursing-home waiting list. Interviews showed that some of the applicants for places in the community service agency's nursing home could live in protective housing, if it were available. Mindful of the group homes organized for other fragile populations—mentally and physically handicapped people and children in need of supervision—the agency's board decided to attempt a similar project for the elderly. Keeping the project in the city made it easier to utilize agency and nursing-home personnel and programs; for example, some of Valdene's residents enjoy attending the senior day-care program at the nursing home. It also satisfied the desire of applicants to remain in the city.

The idea of using apartments instead of a house was novel at the time. Yet the apartments were available, and there was no valid reason for not using them for a group-sharing arrangement.

Valdene opened in 1979 with room for twelve residents in four apartments. Although not fully rented until the end of the first year, another apartment was later added for three more residents, and there is now a waiting list of six. "Most of those who moved in might otherwise have gone into nursing homes. Not because they needed such extensive care, but because they were no longer able to cope with the trials and tribulations of living alone," according to Valdene's resident manager, Roslyn D——. She also pointed out that the arrangement saves scarce nursing-home places for those in real need of the care. "Not that some of our residents don't have to make the move sooner or later. But being here extends their time of independence. And the longer we can help them do that, the better."

Lily was a prime example of the possibilities for prolonging independence in this supportive environment. At 92, partially deaf, almost blind, and having suffered a major heart attack, she had been living at Valdene for five years. Every day was still exciting for her. She attended the senior day-care program, driven to and fro in Valdene's van. She called the program her club and was so enthusiastic about it that she had enticed several of her fellow residents into joining the program. "I always keep my pocketbook, hat, and gloves handy on the dresser near the door, so I'm ready to go out whenever anyone invites me on an outing," Lily said.

Her bedroom was neat and uncluttered, seeming to have a place for everything. This had been the master bedroom of one of the self-contained apartments and had its own bath. The other two bedrooms' residents shared a bath and, therefore, paid slightly lower rents. All apartments came furnished, but each resident added some personal items.

Lily's apartment mates, Rachel and Jenny, were in the kitchen preparing lunch for themselves. Jenny, 85 and with bad arthritis, held on to counters as she moved awkwardly around the room. Her cane hung over one of the chairs.

The refrigerator and cabinets were kept stocked by the manager and her assistants, with reasonable requests by residents taken into account when the weekly shopping list was compiled. Residents able to do some shopping could, of course, pick up extras for the meals they prepared themselves—breakfast and lunch—and for snacking.

Was there dissension in the kitchen? "Not always," was Rachel's answer, followed by the laughter of the other two women. "It's hard to get used to sharing and working with other people around. But you soon learn." Jenny added proudly, "I think we three get along better than any of the others."

Jenny, the most recent arrival, seemed the most well adjusted. She claimed that she regarded Lily and Rachel as sisters. Yet she had been very resistant to the move from her own home. Widowed two years before after 62 years of marriage, she had plunged into a deep depression. "I was completely demolished. A nervous wreck. I couldn't drive, and that was like losing my right arm."

Her sons, both living some distance away, came to visit as often as they could after the death of their father. "They worried about me and tried to get me to move nearer to them. And I worried about them, because they're getting older, too, and it was hard for them to make the trip. But I had no intention of moving," Jenny explained.

Even after visiting Valdene at the suggestion of a social worker and finding the place pleasant and the people friendly, the idea of living with strangers upset Jenny. "How do you ask a total stranger to zip up your dress?" she had wondered. "What I didn't realize," she acknowledged, "is that when you live together, you don't stay strangers for very long."

At the urging of her sons, she finally consented to a one-month trial, certain that she would return to her home afterward. "But a very strange thing happened. The morning after my first night here, I went into the kitchen, and instead of saying, 'Good morning, stove. Good morning, sink. Good morning, table,' I said, 'Good morning, Lily. Good morning, Rachel.' And best of all, they said, 'good morning' back to me."

Rachel nodded her head in agreement. "That's the main thing— not being alone. I lived alone for eleven years, first in my house, then in an apartment. It's so frightening to feel sick at night with no one there," she said sadly.

Rachel was 86 years old, a former school teacher. She had suffered a series of small strokes after her husband's death, and she came to Valdene using a walker that now stood in a corner of her room, used only on days when she felt "real shaky." Her assessment of Valdene: "Life here isn't bad, but it's not a bed of roses. We're all set in our ways, and we get on each other's nerves sometimes. One plays her TV too loud. One clops around in the kitchen at night when she can't sleep. One leaves crumbs all over the living room.

"On the other hand," Rachel continued, "it's good to know there's someone here to talk to or if you get sick suddenly. You feel a lot safer. And it takes the strain off your children."

"That's absolutely true," declared Jenny. "I used to call my sons ten times a day sometimes. Such phone bills! And what could they do, so far away? I remember my youngest once saying, 'Ma, you're driving me crazy. You have to let us bring you out here or find someone there to take care of you.' I'm ashamed now. But I just couldn't help myself then. I needed to know they were still there."

Lily smiled at them forbearingly. She had been a widow for 40 years, almost half of her life, and had lived in many places. She had shared a friend's home in Florida for many years until the friend died, after which she moved back to the city to be near her three children, all of whom lived within a ten-mile radius of her apartment. Seeking peer companions, she entered the nursing home's day-care program while still living alone in her apartment. Only after she experienced a bad fall could her son and daughter convince her to move into the group apartments; the other son opposed the move, preferring that she stay in her own home with full-time help.

Lily chose Valdene. "I like being with people. And I can still come and go as I please, just as I did in my old apartment. I don't mind sharing part of the apartment as long as I have one room to myself. I'm happy not to have to do any heavy cleaning or cooking anymore. And I enjoy having my evening meal on the 16th floor with all the others. Reminds me of a college dorm. I don't think I could manage nearly as well by myself without a lot of help from my children. And the last thing I want to do is be a burden to them—they've got enough problems of their own. So there we are. I really feel lucky to be here."

Had the dissenting son changed his mind? Lily said she thought so, but suggested we ask him ourselves.

"Basically, no," asserted Elliot, Lily's 68-year-old son, a lawyer with a successful private practice. "Any arrangement is second best compared to living alone. That may be my own prejudice speaking, of course. My mother is very sociable and very tolerant. So far, she's been able to maintain that delicate balance between sharing and complete dependence. And she definitely needs some kind of supervision but is much too lively to be put into a nursing home—that might have killed her. Valdene seems to be good for her. In that it has relieved me and my sister and brother of some anxiety, it has also been good for us."

Elliot's views on Valdene are closer than he imagined to those of other residents' sons and daughters. Half the women who lived there chose Valdene for themselves, then sold the idea to their children; the other half had been persuaded by their children, according to manager Roslyn D———. Most children and parents finally agreed, a helpful factor in the resident's adjustment, which usually occurred within a period of two months. The biggest problem, according to

Roslyn, was that by the time an applicant and her family were ready
to accept group living, the old person was often too frail or impaired
to be accepted.

"As it is, we have a very old population here. Average age is 86,
probably due to our original intake of people just this side of nursing-
home admission. Many of them have continued to live here, while
others have had to move on to the nursing home or have passed on.
Our ladies don't like to talk about those who leave—they find it depressing. And they shouldn't have to face these losses as often as they
do. It would be better if we had a younger mix.

"It would be nice to have a few men residents, too," Roslyn
added. "But we've never had three men apply at the same time, and
we're reluctant to have men and women share one apartment."

Roslyn also deplored the reduction in resident participation
caused by the frailties of advanced age. "Valdene was founded on the
idea that shared living would encourage independence by pooling
the unused resources and strengths of older people so they could run
cooperative households with only minimal help from us. Instead,
there's more dependence than we expected, and staff and services
have had to increase over the years." She pointed to that dependence
as one reason for the $300 increase in monthly charges during the
seven years Valdene had been in operation: from $425 for a room
with shared bath and $525 for a room with private bath to $725 and
$825, respectively.

Having seen three shared group homes, we have some insight
into how this kind of living arrangement works. We know the homes
are tenanted by people of diverse backgrounds and interests, brought
together by circumstance rather than by affinity. What they have in
common are economic, physical, and emotional problems that make
it difficult or impossible for them to live alone. For the majority,
living with children is not an acceptable solution, although they
want to live close enough for regular visits and for help in case of
serious illness.

It is obvious that group-sharing participants must have a decent
level of tolerance for the foibles of others and enough flexibility to
trade some privacy for companionship, concern, and support. Con-

tinued family attention is important for successful adaptation to the change in lifestyle; without it, the older person may feel bitter and abandoned. Most children understand this need and faithfully maintain contact with their parents during and after the period of adjustment. In fact, adult children and parents seem to derive greater pleasure from their relationships once the elders are no longer solely dependent on the children and the anxieties and uncertainties are eased.

There are differences between the three group homes we visited. Except for location, however, these are mainly differences in degree. Grove Cottage is set up for the greatest self-reliance, Valdene for the least. Grove Cottage and Parkside (indeed, most group homes) include men, Valdene does not. Most of these differences stem from the characteristics of the population served by each home: age, physical ability, values, experience. Perhaps city people, like Valdene's residents, are more accustomed to a wide range of services in their homes than are people from suburban and rural areas.

Essentially, shared group homes all have the same purpose: to offer the frail, perhaps somewhat impaired elderly a chance to extend their years of independence in a family setting and in clean, safe, affordable housing rooted in the community. The community benefits by the efficient use of existing housing stock, reduced pressure on costly community resources (nursing homes, hospitals, social-service agencies), and the stability and experience old people bring to a community.

Perhaps the most exciting aspect of shared group housing is that the concept lends itself to almost infinite variation. Any group—large or small, rich or poor, urban or suburban—can develop a plan best suited to its members and their community. In other words, any one of us, seeing or foreseeing the need, can form the nucleus of a group to start a shared-living home.

# 3

# For the Rest of My Life— Or Almost

*Life-care and other congregate communities*

A PLAY called "I'm Not Rappaport," popular on Broadway in the 1980s, dealt with old age and its challenges. The playwright, Herb Gardner, showed us a man of strong political passions undiminished by his 80-plus years who battled against ageism and a multitude of other "isms."

In the struggle to retain his individuality and freedom, Rappaport even lashed out at his own daughter when she presented him with three choices: to live at her house in the suburbs, to move to a senior citizens' housing complex, or to give up his park bench and attend the neighborhood senior center where he would be provided with a hot lunch and planned activities each day. His response was "OK, we got three possibilities. We got Siberia. We got Devil's Island. And we got kindergarten." At first, he rejected them all. Later, he relented and went to the senior center.

Despite his scorn for senior housing and senior centers, a real-life Rappaport would probably be the first to fight for the rights of the elderly should these services be threatened. Furthermore, had Rappaport made the trip to one nearby "Devil's Island," he might have been astonished at how much freedom, independence, and purposeful activity many of his contemporaries enjoyed there.

Only a short bus ride from Rappaport's park bench is one of the oldest congregate residences in the eastern United States. A 15-story building with 250 studio and one-bedroom apartments, Feld House is about 30 years old. Each resident pays a monthly fee that covers rent for an apartment, two meals per day (noon and evening), housekeeping services, and a variety of social, recreational, and cultural programs. The residents, who must be over 62 and ambulatory, bring their own furnishings to the apartments. And they have the privacy of these individual living units and the freedom to come and go as they please for as long as their health and strength hold out— sometimes longer, with the help of their fellow tenants.

Rappaport might have liked living at Feld House. It is in a busy uptown section, a mixed working- and middle-class neighborhood with stores, a bank, a luncheonette—all good places to stop and talk. A park two blocks away has ranks of benches that are lively with conversation in good weather. At Feld House he would have found people actively engaged in neighborhood life—as political- and social-club members and as hospital and social-agency volunteers.

Dora had lived at Feld House for five years and was 81 when we met her. Rappaport would probably have liked her. She loved to argue about politics, and she was a staunch defender of the rights of the underdog.

Before coming to live at Feld House, Dora lived in a two-bedroom apartment in the downtown area of the city. The mother of three children and with no professional training, she became involved in school parent organizations, the neighborhood association, her local political club, and a hospital women's auxiliary. Dora was 54 when her husband, an insurance broker, died. To counteract the loneliness, she shared her apartment with a single woman, an arrangement that lasted for many years until Dora fell and broke her right hip and began having problems with housekeeping and shopping.

Dora's daughter, Shirley, described her mother as a "superefficient housekeeper." She said, "It drove her up the wall to be at home and not be able to do things with her usual polish and finesse."

Shirley recounted how her mother had first seen Feld House when a friend moved there. Dora had applied on the spot without discussing her decision with Shirley and her two brothers, all of whom lived in the metropolitan area. "I don't mind telling you, we thought she was off her rocker—that maybe her arthritis had reached her brain. Otherwise, we said, why would she sign herself into an old-age home?

Shirley smiled at the recollection of how they had tried to persuade Dora to stay in her old apartment. "I felt rotten about her moving for two reasons. First of all, it was my childhood home she was abandoning. Secondly, I didn't think she was so old and feeble that she belonged in an institution yet. It's a good thing she didn't listen to us. It would have meant a lot of work and worry for me if she had stayed where she was. And who knows, she might have had to go into a nursing home."

Dora's determination and adaptability made for a fairly easy transition to a congregate lifestyle. She joined several organizations and became involved in activities new to her, such as painting and choral singing. "I can't tell you how much joy I get out of doing the painting and singing. It's wonderful, at my age, to have discovered these new worlds. Lately, I've missed one or two chorus rehearsals—a little tired, or lazy maybe. But the painting I can do right here in my apartment, even when I don't get down to classes," Dora said.

Her appreciation of the cleanliness, order, and good meals was effusive. If it had been necessary for her to struggle along every day doing all those things for herself, Dora stressed, she would never have had the energy for the stimulating new hobbies and friendships. "As it is, no matter how stiff and creaky I feel, I'm glad to get up every morning."

A day at Feld House begins early for most of its residents. Dora said she awoke at first light most mornings: "But I hug my pillow until my mind frees itself from the cobwebs. Then I like to think about my plans for the day until the juices start flowing."

After a warm shower, Dora prepared a "bit of breakfast" for herself. "I've never liked having a big breakfast. A little fruit juice, a cup of coffee, a slice of toast—that's enough for me," she explained, adding that she was grateful the morning meal was not part of the service package. "Old people need to go at their own pace in the morning."

Dora recalled how she had polled the residents soon after she moved into the house, hoping enough of them would agree with her that lunch should be changed to an optional meal as well. Although almost half of the 268 residents approved of the change, management regarded the midday meal as too important to be left to the vagaries of the residents. Dora half-heartedly agreed: "I guess they realized some of us eat very little breakfast and might skimp on lunch, or even forget about it. But that was one of the hardest things to get used to at the beginning—eating meals at the same time every day. I never liked doing it before."

"Oh, Momma," Shirley teased, "when you lived alone, you often forgot meals altogether."

A few residents did eat breakfast in the main dining room between 8:00 and 9:30: residents who were disoriented and confused, whose kitchenette stoves had been disconnected, and anyone who wanted an occasional change. Sunday pancake breakfasts drew a large crowd. The charge for these meals was minimal.

Perhaps one-fourth of the residents were out of the building at lunchtime on days with decent weather, perhaps on an excursion with family, friends, or a Feld House group, or at a job. Most of these jobs were volunteer work, but a very few holdovers still went off to paying jobs. In her first few years at Feld House, Dora worked as a volunteer teacher's aide, two days a week, in a neighborhood elementary school. She later reduced her schedule to one day a week, then found her arthritis made it too painful to continue.

"How I miss the little ones," she sighed. "The teachers bring them here to visit or for a concert now and then, but it's not the same as being with them for hours and having them turn to you for help or just for a hug. Ah, if only I could paint the light, the wonder, in those eyes . . . "

These days, Dora said, she spent more of her time in Feld House. After breakfast, she made her bed, tidied the already neat bedroom and living room, finished dressing, and headed downstairs. The elevator on her side of the building was only a few doors from her apartment. On the way, she tapped softly on one of the doors with her cane. "Is that you, Dora?" a woman's voice called. At Dora's affirmative answer, the woman opened the door.

"How are you this morning, Bessie?" Dora asked.

"I think I'll live the day," answered the other woman.

"Good!" Dora said cheerily. "So I'll see you downstairs."

By the time the elevator reached the eighth floor where Dora waited, it was half-full of residents from the upper floors. By the time it reached ground level, it was full of people greeting each other and exchanging a few words.

In the large lobby, decorated with paintings and needlework done by the residents, newspapers were piled on a table opposite the receptionist's office counter. The night receptionist was still there, talking to the woman who came on duty at 8:30. They were both greeted warmly by the residents, some of whom were leaving the building, and they responded in kind.

Dora and several other residents took a newspaper from the table and went through an open double doorway into the lobby lounge, where they sat and read the papers. A few residents returned to the elevators to read the papers in their own apartments. Except for two copies of the major newspapers ordered by Feld House for its library, residents paid for their individual subscriptions.

About one-half hour later, Bessie joined Dora in the lounge, where she was listening to another woman's earnest conversation. After a few minutes of three-way discussion, Dora asked, "We have about three-quarters of an hour before art class. Should we go out for a walk?"

The other two women declined. "It's chilly out, so we'd have to go up and get our coats," said one.

"Let's go out this afternoon. I need some stockings, so we can walk over to the discount store near the bank," Bessie suggested. They all agreed and sat and discussed the newspaper headlines and other matters until it was time to take the elevator to the floor below. There they strolled down the corridor, past the utility rooms, maintenance department, housekeeping offices, and supply rooms to the large studio room with its easels and work tables.

Dora went to a closet for her paint box and a partially completed canvas. The other two women went into an adjacent room where the long tables were laden with yarns of every imaginable color, a few needlepoint frames, and a table with colored tissue paper and ingenious constructions of exotic birds and flowers.

Beyond the crafts area was the residents' laundry room, with bags and baskets of laundry at various stages of completion. Only a few residents waited on metal folding chairs—reading, watching the machines, or dozing.

The rest of the space on the lower level was occupied by the auditorium, with a piano on one side and just below the small stage at the far end. Here resident council meetings were held at least once each month. Subcommittees met in the library, crafts area, or lounges, but full council meetings were held in the auditorium, as were films, concerts, choir practice, and parties.

The dining room was situated above the auditorium on the street floor at the opposite end from the lobby. At lunchtime, it was noisy until the food was served. Then people ate quietly, concentrating on the food and the mechanics of holding the cup steady and keeping the fork from slipping out of arthritic fingers, only occasionally conversing with fellow diners. The room, a pleasant blend of pastel pink and green, was clean and fairly quiet, and the food was good.

After lunch, residents again went their separate ways: some out to the terrace, with its pots of geranium and balsam, to sit in the afternoon sun; others went to the game room to play cards, Scrabble, checkers, or chess; others left the building to walk, shop, and do errands. Many, including Dora and Bessie, returned to their apartments to watch television, to nap, or both.

The two women agreed to meet an hour later for their neighborhood walk. When they returned, Dora would go to choir practice if she was not too tired. A small group of choristers regularly sang for nursing-home patients as well as at Feld House functions and at religious services in the Chapel. Occasionally the full choral group gave a joint concert with a neighborhood school chorus at an assembly. Bessie, who was a once-a-week volunteer for the resident-run notions shop, would spend the last two hours before dinner on duty there.

After dinner and perhaps an hour of conversation in one of the lounges or a short stroll on nearby streets, most people retreated to their apartments to read, sew, watch television, and prepare for bed. Most days were quite full. "I'm often tired at the end of the day," said Dora, "but I'm never bored."

Before we left Feld House, Shirley introduced us to Mary, her mother's 90-year-old sister. Mary had moved from her old apartment into a studio unit at Feld House two years before, but was still not accustomed to the residence. Her eyes were pink-rimmed, as though she cried often, and she had an angry, suspicious look on her face, even after her niece kissed her and greeted her affectionately.

Later, Shirley theorized that her aunt's unhappiness grew from her personality and from her advanced age when she moved in. A woman with little education and few interests outside her home, Mary had derived her greatest satisfaction from being a good housewife, cook, and hostess. She was also an attentive and devoted mother to her four children. They returned her devotion, especially the two daughters who cared for Mary during the previous decade as her health declined.

"Both of them at her apartment every day—cleaning, fetching and carrying, bathing her," Shirley said. "Then one of my cousins became seriously ill. Cancer. Her sister tried to take care of her and her mother, but it was an awful strain. We'd persuaded Mary to sign up here years ago, right after my mom moved in. But she balked every time an apartment was free. Now there's a five-year waiting list. Luckily an apartment became available when the family really needed it."

So the move had been made in desperation, at an age when Mary would probably have been happier staying in her old home with a homemaker/companion or practical nurse. Given her personality and interests, it would have been difficult for Mary to relate to most of the other residents and to adjust to congregate living at any age. Had she been 10 or 15 years younger, however, she might have had the energy and will to make a few friends and to derive some pleasure from the social life at Feld House.

Shirley added a sad note, saying, "My cousin, Mary's oldest daughter, died last year. Her family is very bitter. They say Mary made her life miserable. They go so far—which is foolish of course—as to blame the illness on poor old Mary."

By contrast, Shirley said, her mother had been sensible and self-reliant. "I've realized for a long time how wise Mom was to move to Feld while she still had the energy and health to enjoy the activities. It wouldn't be too easy for her now, her arthritis has gotten so bad. And all this while, my brothers and I have been assured that she's safe and eating well, seeing her doctor, and taking her medication. I wonder what would have happened to all of us if she had tried to stick it out alone in her apartment all these years? A lot of work and worry," she mused.

In a southeastern town, Linda worried about her mom, Susan, who was several thousand miles away in the Northwest. Susan had moved from a large suburban house to a city apartment soon after her husband, a machine-tool manufacturer, died. The move was very traumatic. "She was 76," said Linda, "and her whole life was centered in my father and that house. She felt lost. She dropped out of the country club and her whole social set. She had the car and could still drive wherever she wanted to, but she rarely went out."

A severe heart attack, then frequent fainting spells, sent Susan to the hospital repeatedly. At home she had household help but was alone at night. Linda and her sister, who lived in eastern Canada, flew out to see their mother as often as they could. Between times, they worried. They tried desperately to convince Susan to move in with one of them, but she refused. "I never want to move again!" she declared fervently. It was an impasse.

Meanwhile, a good friend took Linda along on a visit to her mother, who had recently moved to a life-care community on the edge of town. Before we learn about the visit and its consequences, a brief pause for explanations.

A *life-care community* (which may also be called a *continuing care retirement community*) is congregate housing that includes a contract for lifetime health care. In *congregate housing*, residents live in apartments, ranging from studio to one- and two-bedroom units, which are especially designed with safety features for the elderly, such as grab bars in the bathroom and emergency buzzers throughout. Each resident has a separate, self-contained unit with bath, kitchen, sleeping area, and living room; the kitchen may be only a small wall or corner assembly, and in a studio/efficiency unit, living and sleeping spaces are combined.

These apartments can be in high-rise, low-rise, or campus-style cottage buildings. The buildings are usually new and may be in city, town, suburban, or rural areas. However, they may be renovated older buildings, such as unused school, factory, office, or private estate buildings. Called *rehabs*, these transformed, cast-off structures enjoyed a short-lived popularity for community use as low- and 'moderate-income senior housing in the early 1970s and 1980s. Apparently more profitable as luxury condominium, office, and commercial complexes, rehabs are now less frequently used for senior housing.

Communal spaces at congregate residences are provided for dining, recreational, and social activities. The monthly fee includes apartment rental, at least one meal per day, housekeeping, linen service, recreational and cultural programs, and 24-hour emergency assistance. Congregate communities usually do not charge an entry fee and do not include lifetime health and nursing care, whereas entry fees paid upon acceptance into a life-care community cover all levels of care that the resident may need in the future. The contract between each incoming resident and the life-care community guarantees health care until the end of the resident's life, except for any periods of hospitalization. Many newer life-care communities offer the additional advantage of a refund of up to 95 percent of the entry fee either to the individual who leaves the community or to her estate.

Feld House is a congregate community, offering only emergency medical care. Although it is affiliated with a nearby nursing home by virtue of both facilities having the same sponsor, this is not the rule.

Ridgecrest, the new home of Linda's friend's mother, is a life-care community. Operated by a church-sponsored nonprofit corporation, it must nevertheless charge a substantial entry fee to maintain residential and skilled nursing services and still remain solvent.

Clusters of attractive one- and two-bedroom cottages, two lodge-type buildings—each with a dozen studio units—a large, barnlike building used as a dining and meeting hall, and a long, two-story brick building that contains the health-related and skilled nursing facilities make up the Ridgecrest Retirement Residence. Linda thought it idyllic. And her friend's mother, though a new arrival, was full of praise for the place and the people who, she said, were lively, interesting, and friendly. The apartments seemed well designed, nicely decorated (unfurnished) with carpeting and draperies, roomy, and well ventilated.

The visitors joined residents for lunch and found the dining room bright and cheerful, with large windows facing the wooded grove at the edge of the community's property. Linda thought the food and service were quite good, too. Before she left, she picked up a descriptive brochure and an application to take to her mother the next time she flew out to see her.

"It wasn't easy getting Mother to fill out the form. She insisted she never wanted to have to move again," Linda recalled. "But I told her there was a four-year wait and no compulsion to accept an apartment if and when there was an opening. It was like insurance, I said.

But I don't think Mother ever gave it another thought until her best friend died suddenly."

It was another hard blow for Susan. Fainting episodes became more frequent. She stopped driving her car and went nowhere. Her resistance to moving shattered, she no longer cared where or whether she lived. Linda brought Susan home to live with her, hoping that an apartment would soon be available at Ridgecrest.

Leaving her job as office manager at a brokerage firm, Linda attempted to cheer her mother with shopping trips, activities at a local country club, and evenings out with family friends. "After many months, Mother began to perk up a little. But as soon as she felt better, she refused to go out with us. With no friends of her own, that meant sitting home alone and brooding. One night, Jeff and I came home and found her stretched out on the living room floor in a faint," Linda recalled. "But she was terribly insulted when we offered to get a sitter the next time we had a date. So we stopped going out unless she went with us. It was hard on our social life. And we didn't take a vacation trip that year, either."

Linda downplayed her feelings of relief when an apartment became available at Ridgecrest. And, in truth, she spent a great deal of time with her mother even after Susan had moved into the one-bedroom cottage unit. As Susan remembered it more than a year later, "I could accept the move intellectually but not emotionally. I didn't make any effort to be friendly or to join in any of the activities. If it were up to me, I'd have stayed in the cottage all day. But management insists you come to the dining room for dinner every evening. And Linda came almost every day and dragged me out—to play bridge, to go to special luncheons and meetings. Now I belong to a regular bridge group. And I've joined a few committees and found some friends I really feel comfortable with."

According to Linda, Susan's fainting spells had stopped, her general health had improved, and she had become involved in a book-discussion group, the county art society, the residents' trip-planning committee, and volunteer desk work at the town birth-control clinic. "Best of all," Linda said proudly, "she looks more animated now than she has at any time since my dad died."

Susan commented, "I do think this is a lovely place. And I guess I can truthfully say that, at last, I feel at home here. But what can I say about my darling daughter except that I'm so very grateful that she never gave up on me."

Some congregate communities, like Feld House, and most life-care communities, like Ridgecrest, are expensive, and anyone considering this living arrangement must have savings or assets, such as a house or other property, and income sufficient to pay the entry and monthly fees. Someone with a low fixed income, to whom this alternative appeals, might choose instead to apply for an apartment in a *government-subsidized housing project for the elderly*. A few of these projects have congregate service programs subsidized by federal or state funds and partly paid for by residents, either by flat fee or on a sliding scale based on income. Subsidized housing with congregate services may also be referred to as *enriched housing*. By either name, these programs are the exception rather than the rule; the majority of subsidized-housing residents make do without the congregate services, rely on younger family members or other neighbors, or turn to community social agencies for needed services.

One special housing project in a small midwestern city is called Avery Square Apartments. It consists of 85 apartments housing 98 elderly tenants in four three-story buildings ranged around an open court with a small park at its center. Twenty-one of the residents receive congregate services that include one meal per day, housekeeping, and personal services as needed. Personal services might include help with bathing, getting dressed, care of clothing, and shopping.

An 86-year-old woman, Elinor, is one resident who could not have stayed in her apartment without the extra household help and meals. Her body misshapen by arthritis, she leaned heavily on her walker as she showed us around her apartment: a small kitchen and bedroom facing the walkway between two buildings; a windowless bathroom with grab bar, stall shower, and emergency buzzer cord; and an average-sized living room with two windows overlooking the court. Tastefully furnished with items that wore the patina of years of use, the room was clean and pleasant.

"When I moved in nine years ago, I could still do the cleaning, shopping, and cooking by myself. But after about five years, I couldn't manage very well anymore. I don't know what I'd do if I couldn't get the extra help," Elinor said. "I just know I'd never want to move in with any of my friends or my children."

Elinor, who had never married, had been a teacher and administrator at several children's homes before retiring. She liked to refer to her former students as her children, and she still kept in touch with some of them. Two who took a special interest in her through the years she regarded as her sons, though the adoption had never been formalized by law. Elinor had no other family.

"The boys," she explained, had urged her to apply for an apartment at Avery Square while the project was under construction. For many years before that, she had shared a small house on the outskirts of the city with a friend. When the friend died, Elinor tried to find another housemate, without success. First, there was a graduate student who often had men friends staying with her, played loud music, and came home in the early morning hours. Several additional housemates were unacceptable, probably because the house was small and the fixed habits of the owner clashed with those of her tenants. But without someone to share mortgage, taxes, and other household expenses, Elinor could not survive on her Social Security and meager savings.

"My boys offered to help out. And I had friends who wanted me to come and live with them. But I preferred to live independently, as I always have," Elinor stated. Continuing with her account of her search for a satisfactory living arrangement, she told how she had investigated several life-care and congregate communities in the area. "There was one I especially liked, but it was much too expensive. I just couldn't afford it," she said.

In general, though, Elinor was pleased with her life at Avery Square. She was active on the tenants' council, frequently went on trips planned by and for the seniors, played bingo in the afternoon, and made a point of walking twice around the park on the days she did not walk the two blocks to the neighborhood shopping center. A nearly blind neighbor accompanied Elinor on these walks. They reinforced each other's resolve to walk. Considering how laborious all Elinor's movements were, these walks seemed an act of courage.

In her parting words about Avery Square, Elinor emphasized the advantages of the project's small size. "A larger project would be confusing. Here, even though it takes all of us time to learn to cope with our new surroundings, it's easier. It takes less time to begin to feel at home."

The Avery Square project was also home to 83-year-old Diana. Born and having lived all her life in Yorkshire, England, Diana came to the United States after her husband's death at the insistence of her only child, Edwina. In her early 20s Edwina married an American professor who had been visiting the university she attended; she then left England and her parents for a home in the United States. Regular visits were exchanged over the years, and the relationship between parents, children, and then grandchildren remained warm and close.

"When my dad died, everything was shattered. Mum had depended on him for everything. There wasn't much money. He'd only been a state-school teacher, and she'd earned a little giving piano lessons. And the old house was falling down 'round their ears. Both getting on in years, you know. Then Dad's being so ill and all. It really sent Mum into an awful state of depression," Edwina recalled.

"It was a terrible time," her mother corroborated. "There was I, an old woman just past my 75th birthday. Never so alone in my life. And my only child 3,000 miles away! My thoughts were only of death, that's all. I just flat out wanted to die."

Edwina was having none of that, however. She knew that her mother had been well and strong during the year her father was invalided by stroke, and she suspected that the morbidity Diana professed was mainly psychological. Determined to bring her mother back home with her, Edwina went to Yorkshire where she arranged her mother's affairs, disposed of the house and most of its furnishings, and packed and shipped the most precious possessions, including Diana's piano. She returned with her unresistant mother. For the next four years, Diana lived in Edwina's home but showed only slight improvement in her mental state.

"It really is not good for the old to live with the young," Diana commented. "I felt very strongly that I should have a place of my own. I wanted to be near Edwina and the family, of course, but I didn't want to live in their house."

Edwina yielded to her mother's wishes, and they looked for suitable living quarters. Avery Square, only a few miles from the house Edwina and her husband had occupied for almost 30 years, had a 2-year waiting list. Diana applied for an apartment but continued looking. She and Edwina wandered farther afield, but always came back to Avery Square. "It seemed the most practical in location, set-up, and cost. So in spite of Mum's impatience to be on her own, we waited it out—about two and a half years!—until an apartment was free.

"Not that I minded," Edwina hastened to add, "I thought all along that it was fine having her live with us. It's a large house, lots of room. Never could quite fathom why Mum was so anxious to leave."

Nevertheless, Edwina helped her mother move and settle into the small apartment (very like neighbor Elinor's). Although Diana did not need the congregate services as yet, both mother and daughter appreciated knowing she could apply for them in the future. After only a short time, Edwina noticed a change. Diana, who had scarcely touched the piano since her husband's death, began practicing in her own living room. Later she played for fellow residents in the common room, then accepted the job of accompanist at church choir rehearsals. Her social life brightened considerably, too, and she began seeing new friends, inviting them to lunch or afternoon tea and invited by them in return.

"I can scarcely believe my eyes sometimes. Is this the same sad lady who moped around my house? It's really quite wonderful how her real spirit and lively nature have returned since she moved to Avery Square," Edwina exclaimed.

Each of the octogenarians in this chapter has a unique personality and life story, but a common thread binds them to each other and to many other aging Americans. Impelled by circumstance to change their customary patterns of living, they all rejected the option of living with children. They seemed to say, My independence is as important to me as my children's independence is to them.

Not so long ago, moving into a child's home was one of the most likely options for an old person no longer able to live alone. But the elderly's claim to independence has strengthened in the past few decades, buttressed by improved economic security and the political punch implicit in greater numbers. To maintain this cherished independence, an older person may cling to her home long after the ability to care for the home and for herself has waned. For her, more than for most younger people, home represents not only physical possessions, but also security and a link to the past. Loosening the grip on this life center is disorienting at the very least, and it may be terrifying for both the aging parent and the adult child. But once the break has been made, as we have seen, the child is instrumental in helping the parent achieve the highest level of independence possible.

Sometimes the parent will take the initiative, as Dora did by entering Feld House long before her children thought it necessary. In her case, the family had to be convinced. More often the parent needs convincing, as did the other three women, who needed varying degrees of coaxing by their children before they agreed to the change. But all of them seemed to trust their children, to be willing to take their advice, and to be without fear of losing their affection and loyalty. Maintaining good relations between older parents and adult children was of paramount importance to most of those with whom we spoke. And there were definite indications that such relations improved when the problem of where the elderly parent could safely live had been resolved.

Frail old people on the verge of dependency are not the only ones who benefit from congregate living. Many of the younger elderly who adopt this lifestyle say they feel more secure, free, and happy than many of their counterparts living alone: less fearful of criminal attack or of sudden illness with no one near to help, free from the energy drain of heavy housework and meal preparation, and blessed with greater opportunities for friendship and stimulating activities.

Couples, too, are discovering the advantages of congregate living arrangements. One woman, writing of her experience, described how she and her husband planned their move from their Connecticut home to a life-care community in Pennsylvania.[1] "The time came when my husband, and then I, decided to stop driving. This . . . meant we would have to look into new living arrangements. Although our daughter and son-in-law suggested building an apartment for us in the garden of their suburban home, we thought we should look into retirement communities."

Although they had friends who had resettled in such communities, the Hales felt none they had seen met their particular needs or their desire to live in the countryside in an area of hilly terrain. When a neighbor loaned them a brochure about a new life-care community, they visited and liked what they saw, including the site on a lake and surrounded by wildlife preserves.

Mrs. Hale wrote about their move: "It proved to be the wisest decision we ever made. We found a place where all our needs were met—a spacious apartment with a view, a medical center that provided complete care, proximity to a fine hospital, nourishing meals attractively served, 24-hour security, transportation for shopping, and friendly, congenial people. There was a pervading air of sincere caring by both staff and members."

At this life-care community, the monthly fee was based on the type of apartment, the number of occupants and the amount of the down payment. The cost was substantial. But the Hales "were pleased to learn that the IRS allows a generous percentage of the monthly fee as a medical deduction."

During their first year at the community, the couple participated in all activities—lectures, concerts, trips, and sports. We took long walks and danced at parties and made many good friends." Then Mr. Hale underwent surgery, followed by a broken hip, which curtailed his activity. After a few months in the community's medical center, however, he was able to return to the apartment and to live there for three more years with the aid of a walker. When it became necessary for him to have nursing care, Mrs. Hale felt "he received more loving care there [at the medical center] than he would have received in the usual nursing home." Daily visits were easier, too, as the nursing facility was on the grounds of the life-care community.

To finish the story in Mrs. Hale's words: "When my husband died, I was fortunate to have the support of warm friends. Because many of them have known the pain of bereavement, they were able to help me greatly during a very sad time.

"At 89, I walk about a mile a day, using a cane as a safety measure. The days are never long enough to accomplish all I plan, but each day I give thanks for having found a beautiful place to live and good friends to share it with."

In a society of changing mores and patterns, congregate living for older people is gaining wider acceptance. Though age-specific housing is still frowned on in some quarters, experience has shown that the benefits to the elderly of a communal lifestyle far outweigh any drawbacks. And the most significant of these benefits is the improvement in the quality of life.

By living together in a supportive environment, the elderly are able to avoid or delay entering nursing homes or other health-related facilities where they have less control over their own lives. In addition to meeting many of their physical needs, such as safety, nutrition, and cleanliness, congregate living arrangements enhance the quality of life with stimulating programs and opportunities for friendships. Self-esteem may be raised by involvement in social and community activities in which new roles may be found to replace those lost at retirement.

It is important to remember, however, that only applicants who are ambulatory and in relatively good health are admitted to congregate and life-care residency. For that reason and because specially designed housing is in short supply, it is wise to plan ahead as much as possible. When Linda told her mother to sign up for Ridgecrest as a form of insurance, she was giving her good advice. Waiting periods of four or five years for applicants to good congregate and life-care communities are not uncommon. As for federally subsidized housing projects, in one state alone, New Jersey, there are waiting lists of over 55,000 applicants for approximately 37,000 occupied subsidized senior-citizen housing units.[2]

It is clear that more elderly would opt for specially designed housing and congregate services if more were available. The expensive alternatives—congregate residences and life-care communities—are being constructed and operated by both nonprofit groups and private companies. But construction of subsidized housing has all but subsided now; in fact, federal funding for all new construction, rehabilitation of existing housing, rent subsidies, and congregate housing services programs has been cut sharply.[3]

In some places, state governments are trying to close the gap, but can do very little without federal funds. At Avery Square Apartments, one of the original 62 senior projects in the federal congregate-services countrywide demonstration program, the state took over when the federal government phased out its programs. A few other states have done the same. Tenants were already paying for some services on a sliding scale, and in some projects, the tenant's share of the cost was also increased.

Many residents who had moved into apartments ten years before, when they were in their 70s or 80s, worried about losing the services. By the time they reached their 80s and 90s, they could not have stayed in their apartments were it not for the extra assistance.[4]

Senior advocacy organizations are fighting hard to encourage construction of affordable housing for old and young alike. It has been an uphill, decades-long battle. All who are interested in congregate living arrangements for aging relatives or for themselves ought to join the ranks.

Think about it, Rappaport. It's better than a cold park bench when your bones grow weary but your mind is still sharp. And we need you, Rappaport, to fight the good fight for decent places to live.

# 4

# Your Place and Mine

*Home sharing, accessory apartments, and elder cottages*

THE old adage, "There's nothing new under the sun," like all
adages, is only partly true. But the more you investigate modern living arrangements for the elderly, the more you will discover
how few of the options are new and how many are adaptations from
the past.

Anyone who lived through the depression years of the 1930s in
a poor family will remember having to share a room with siblings in
order to make room for a lodger or boarder. In those days, a space
was often cleared in even the smallest, poorest living quarters for a
paying tenant who received a room and meals or kitchen privileges
for his money. Often the tenant was an immigrant, a single person
newly arrived in this country who needed inexpensive shelter until
he or she could afford a place of his or her own. The lodger helped
the hard-pressed family pay the rent or mortgage payment. No
doubt this mutually beneficial, if somewhat inconvenient, arrangement continues among new immigrant populations. House sharing
by singles and doubling up of families in areas where inexpensive
housing is in short supply are the only ways some people can
manage.

Going back further in history are tales of the penniless widow or
abandoned wife who converted her home into a boarding house in
order to keep a roof over her own head. Indeed, these arrangements
have persisted into the present, for there are boarding homes and
rooming houses for elderly residents; these, too, serve a useful purpose in the spectrum of housing for older people.

More comfortable housing can be found, however, when homeowners are willing to share part or all of their house or apartment

with a tenant. In this regard, a recent and helpful innovation is the *matching agency,* a public or private agency that specializes in matching homeowners with home seekers. By providing a central source of information and some guidance, such agencies expedite the introduction of two segments of the elderly population with meshing needs: the homeowner for additional income, companionship, security, and possibly services; the home seeker for affordable housing, security, and possibly companionship. In addition, many housemate-matching agencies go beyond referrals and introductions, offering counseling and an array of other services for the elderly.

The shared space allotted to a renter may come in several forms: a room or two with bath and use of kitchen and living room in an apartment or house (*home sharing*), a complete apartment in a house (*accessory apartment*), or a separate cottage adjacent to and on the same property as a house (*Elder Cottage Housing Opportunity,* or *ECHO housing,* a name coined by the American Association of Retired Persons, a staunch supporter of this concept).

Zoning restrictions in some towns and cities preclude accessory apartments and ECHO housing in single-family areas, but a growing movement for change in these local laws may alleviate this restraint before too long. In those localities permitting such apartments, other factors have prevented proliferation, mainly (1) the desire for privacy or a lack of knowledge and awareness by homeowners and (2) the expense and inconvenience of conversion. Most often, it is desperation on the part of owners who are financially strapped but determined to keep their homes that compels this course of action.

For Jenny, who had lived in more places than she cared to count, it was fortunate that Dorothy chose to convert the second floor of her pretty saltbox cottage, situated in an area of mixed one- and two-family homes, instead of selling it. Dorothy, the widow of a career naval officer, suffered a sudden drop in income after her husband's death. On the advice of a friend in real estate, she used her husband's life-insurance money to pay for remodeling the upstairs bedrooms into a three-room apartment, keeping the five rooms on the first floor for herself and her precious collection of antiques.

Jenny, at age 76 searching for a place to live, was introduced to Dorothy at the county housing agency where they had both gone for help. Jenny's husband, a barber, had died of a debilitating nerve disease. A gentle and patient woman, she had lovingly nursed him through the last four years of his life while their savings were drained by medical and hospital bills. For that reason she was grateful to her only daughter and son-in-law for putting the couple up, rent free, in a three-room apartment in their two-story home. Soon after the death of Jenny's husband, however, a change of job made it necessary for her son-in-law to sell the house and move his family to a distant part of the state. The couple asked Jenny to move with them, but she wanted to stay in the area where she had spent most of her life.

So Jenny's next move was into a room in her son's apartment in the next town. It was small and crowded. "I didn't mind that so much. I had the place to myself for most of the day. But Mike and Suelee hadn't been married very long, and I felt they needed their privacy," Jenny explained, adding that she had lived in many apartments, some large and some quite small, during her married life.

Then a good friend living in the city lost her husband and asked Jenny to come and stay with her for a while. It was only a three-room apartment, so Jenny slept on the couch in the living room. "It was really quite comfortable. And we talked and cried together, remembering old times. I stayed almost a year, until my friend was ready to move south to a retirement place near her daughter's family," Jenny said.

By that time, Mike had found his mother an inexpensive, one-bedroom garden apartment in town. Though not specifically designed for older people, many of the building's tenants were elderly, and they had formed a good, informal social system—looking out for and helping each other. Jenny was happy there, but after only two years the landlord opted for converting the apartments to condominiums, forcing many of the older tenants to move out.

"That was a blow. For the first time in a long time, I'd allowed myself to feel a sense of permanence," Jenny recalled sadly. "But," she added, "it's all turned out for the best. Because Dorothy was able to convert the upstairs of her house, I have this lovely, roomy apartment. I'm still near my son and Suelee and the children. And I see some of my old friends at the senior center, which I can walk to every day as long as I keep my health. I'm quite content. I just hope I can live here for the rest of my life."

"Amen," chimed in Suelee, who had been standing nearby while her mother-in-law talked. She put her arm around the frail little woman and gave her a hug. The contrast was startling: Suelee was a husky, strapping young woman, usually bare-footed, with a ringing laugh and a direct manner. Her husband, Mike, sometimes called her "Mother Earth."

Talking to us alone later, Suelee said that Jenny was the "dearest, sweetest, most undemanding person—too much so for her own good. I mean, how many old people do you know who have lived through so many changes in late life as she has? And she makes it sound so easy, all those moves. But she was very worried about each one, especially the last. She went so far as to ask Mike and me whether we thought it was a good idea to take a chance on living in such close proximity with a stranger."

The young couple assured her that if she were unhappy, the agency would certainly find her another place to live. "In a worst-case situation, Mom," Mike teased, "you can always move back with us and take care of the three boys."

"Maybe I should," Jenny had said, only half-joking. "I spend so much time with you anyway."

Suelee, now very serious, answered, "And when you do, Mom, you always help in very important ways." Then breaking into a broad grin, she shouted, "Who the heck do you think would do the mending and sewing, the baking and cooking and baby-sitting if it weren't for you?"

Because of this strong family relationship, Jenny did not appear to need the friendship of her landlady. Dorothy, still in her early 60s, had many compelling interests outside of her home; sharing the house with Jenny was strictly a financial matter. Her only concession to neighborliness was to knock on Jenny's door on mornings when she heard no sound of movement upstairs. Also, the two women had exchanged sets of keys and emergency phone numbers and had agreed to notify each other of overnight trips. Otherwise, they led completely separate lives, a situation entirely agreeable to both of them.

Other house sharers and owners form closer relationships. Not long after Vera had moved into the three-room apartment in the G——'s house, the couple began to regard her as family. "Vera is like a sister to me," Rose said, describing how much she and her husband, Tony, liked Vera's company, how they regularly invited her to go shopping with them, and how she and Vera helped each other, exchanging recipes and knitting patterns and soap-opera lore.

Tony, a large, jovial man with a booming voice, agreed. "She's friendly and nice, and we all get along just great," he said.

All three were in their early 70s. Vera, widowed more than 30 years before, had no children. Her only family was a married sister with several children on the West Coast, but Vera had little contact with them. Except for her use of a hearing aid and a slight distortion of speech, she was in good health. She had been for many years head bookkeeper for a wholesale hardware firm, and when she was almost 60 she had returned to school to learn to use computers. Retired at 68, she began to look around for another apartment. The one she had lived in for the previous 14 years, located in a three-family house in the next town, was small and badly in need of repairs that the landlord would not make. The neighborhood, too, had deteriorated.

"I'm eternally grateful to the agency for finding this home for me," Vera exclaimed. "The apartment is so bright and airy and shiny new—and large, too. I can really stretch here. And Rose and Tony are so kind to me. They're the first family I've had in a long time."

Vera was very self-sufficient and spent most of her time alone. Of the few friends she had, none were willing to walk as much as she did; but occasionally they met for lunch, or she invited one or two friends to lunch at her apartment. "I haven't invited people over for years. I was so ashamed of how run-down my old place was," Vera said. Otherwise she took local buses to a shopping mall, art gallery, library, or park.

For Rose and Tony, having a tenant meant, in his words, "keeping this house that we love, our home for 32 years, the place where our son grew up." And the house reflected their love—the neat, red-brick split-level on a small manicured lot with trimmed yews and azaleas around the foundation and privet hedges on both sides separating it from neighboring lots.

Their only living child (one son had died in early childhood) lived a few blocks away with his wife and their three children. Rose and Tony were unusually doting grandparents, and the teenagers frequently stopped in, regarding the house as their second home. Their son, Greg, and his family had encouraged and helped with conversion of the bedroom level into the apartment and the first level to a bedroom and bath for Rose and Tony and another bedroom for guests. Except for moving the staircase to create a separate entrance for the upstairs apartment, the living room, dining room, and kitchen on the midlevel floor stayed the same. The house also had a partly finished basement.

"Plenty of room here. In fact, it's still too large for just two people. My Rose has a bum ticker and she shouldn't even be doing all the housework she does now," Tony said. He then proceeded to describe, with mock horror, the "mess and misery" they experienced during construction. "But I have no regrets," he hastened to assure us. "It was a good move. Not only can we keep the house, but we also have a little extra money now for luxuries, like dinner out once in a while and travel." He mentioned two trips to his ancestral home in Italy and several weekend trips to scenic areas in the countryside with a local senior citizens' club.

Greg was more explicit about his parents' reasons for making the change. "My dad worked as a salesman for a big food company, and he retired with a pretty good pension and his Social Security. That was about seven years ago. But he soon discovered that his money didn't go very far, what with the price of everything, including taxes, going up. Then my mom had her heart attack, and that drained off more money. They were both really scared—about losing the house, about becoming a burden on me. So we came up with this idea for the apartment. And it's worked out real well. Now they feel secure about keeping the house, and they can also enjoy a few luxuries with the extra income."

The house-matching agency contact was made by Greg, who wanted to be certain the renter would be a reputable person. "It may be a separate apartment, but it's still in the same house. And I wanted to be damn careful about who moved in," he said. He also realized, he explained, that if any serious problems developed, the agency could help remove and relocate the tenant, something Rose and Tony would have great difficulty doing by themselves.

For both Vera and the older couple, this proved to be a mutually agreeable and profitable arrangement. Vera had a nice apartment at reasonable rent, plus security and companionship. Rose and Tony gained greater security in their home and some discretionary income to improve the quality of their lives. As Tony said, "The best part is that the house still looks the same outside. And inside, it still feels like *our* house."

Sometimes home seekers are able to trade services for part or all of their rent. Charlotte, a bustling, competent woman of 70, found she could be useful and earn a little money, too, when she agreed to move into Martha's house.

Charlotte and her husband, who had died a short time before, had been government clerks in Washington, D.C. After his death, she sold their house and moved to Ohio to live with her only daughter, Eve, whose husband was an auto mechanic. There were five grandchildren, all nearly grown, and there was much coming and going in the household. Problems arose when Charlotte tried to impose some order on the chaos, thus antagonizing her son-in-law. Enlisting the help of her daughter, she consulted a housemate-matching service.

Martha, age 70, had a completely different life experience and outlook. She had never worked, had always been completely dependent upon her husband (a car dealer), and had enjoyed a degree of luxury Charlotte could only have dreamed about. Martha's only child, a son, had died in an auto accident when he was 40. His only son, Martha's grandson, lived in the southern part of the country; he telephoned and visited only rarely. Her husband's family and her friends were attentive but could not rid her of the depression and confusion that followed her husband's death the year before. The house seemed cavernous, and as Martha said, she felt like a small pebble in a huge, empty drum. When her husband's niece, who lived nearby and worked for a local family-service agency, took her to see the director of the home-share program, she was ready for a housemate. Meanwhile, Charlotte had already visited the agency with her daughter and left an application.

Charlotte had very little money to spend on housing. But Martha did not need the money; she was offering two rooms—sitting room and bedroom with bath—plus the run of the living areas rent free. In addition, she would pay $100 per month in exchange for services.

What Martha hoped for was an efficient house manager to cook, shop, and organize the household. And that's what she found in Charlotte.

Relieved of most household responsibilities, Martha was generous in her praise of Charlotte's competence and good nature. "I'm not very good company these days," she admitted, "but Charlotte is always patient and tries hard to cheer me."

Charlotte said that Martha was often despondent, "though not as often as when I first came to live here. It takes some longer than others to come to terms with the loss of a husband. And when she gets a really bad crying jag, I call her niece or the social worker at the agency."

The social worker called monthly to check on the progress of the pair and to discuss any problems. She seemed to think they were doing very well, although her professional opinion, which she had conveyed earlier to Martha and her niece, was that Martha would have done better to sell her house and move to a congregate or life-care community or to a residential hotel. If Martha chose one of these options, which she could well afford, she would be with women of backgrounds and interests similar to her own. Martha, however, had been adamantly opposed to giving up her house.

In the home-sharing arrangement she chose instead, she and Charlotte were from different socioeconomic backgrounds, and the relationship was more like servant and mistress than one of peer companions. The binding factors in their relationship were almost entirely practical. Martha relied on Charlotte to run her household and as a dependable presence in case of emergency. Charlotte received free room and board and an additional sum every month, all of which were a welcome supplement to her small government pension, enabling her to establish gift funds for her grandchildren, help her daughter with some of the family's disastrous finances, and buy a few extras for herself. She was very pleased with the way things worked out. "My only big wish right now," she concluded, "is for Martha. May the good Lord give her a happier heart."

Where difficult personalities are involved in a home-sharing match, the role of an agency is even more critical. Such was the case with 85-year-old Inez, who came to live with 68-year-old Lucy.

Inez had lived in an apartment with her daughter and son-in-law for 22 years until her daughter developed terminal cancer. When her son-in-law gave up the apartment to move in with his own daughter, Inez hoped to be taken in by one of her other four grandchildren. Distraught over their mother's illness and resentful over what they regarded as her years of sacrifice to Grandmother Inez, none of the grandchildren was willing to have her. They tried but were unable to find an apartment for her in a senior citizens' housing project. An appeal to the regional social-services agency led to a referral to the county housing department's home-matching service.

Realizing that Inez was a dependent person and an unwilling participant in the arrangement, the service tried to choose a younger, more stable homeowner as a partner. This was not an easy task, as there is usually more demand from older owners for younger renters.

Lucy, a recently retired high-school math teacher, had lived in her house for almost 40 years, 10 of them as the widow of a college sociology professor. After her retirement, she found taxes and maintenance of the house too costly and applied to the agency for a home sharer who would have her own bedroom and bath and share the rest of the house. Thus began a rocky relationship.

To begin with, Lucy complained that Inez expected to be waited on. "She wants me to do all the shopping and cooking, to serve the meals and clean up afterward, too. Then she's always asking me to drive her here and there. I didn't ask for a tenant in order to become a housemaid and chauffeur."

Inez appealed for sympathy: "I'm old and sick. I have no strength. I still haven't gotten over this move. I'm ready to have a nervous breakdown. But you won't have to put up with me much longer. My grandchildren are coming for me soon."

With the agency's intervention, Lucy and Inez came to an agreement that was put into writing. Each would shop and cook separately; Inez would be responsible for cleaning her own room, bath, and the kitchen when she used it; Lucy would be responsible for the rest of the house; and Inez would pay Lucy a small sum for transportation.

Three years later, the two were still together, still squabbling over petty annoyances: "Lucy, your cats are on my bed again."

"Inez, I've told you a hundred times to shut your door if you don't want them there."

"Lucy, you left dirty dishes in the sink again last night."

"I was too tired to do them."

"Too drunk, you mean."

And so it went. But like an old married couple, they seemed to have settled into a state of contentious equilibrium—and even to have grown fond of each other.

Would the home-share arrangement have survived the early disagreements without the agency's mediation and the written contract? It's difficult to say. Lucy, the homeowner, might easily have turned Inez back to the agency, creating untold hardships for Inez and her family.

The grandchildren were pleased with the arrangement, despite all Inez's early complaints. "Grandma's a much nicer person now," her granddaughter claimed. "Being with Lucy has made her stand up for herself, instead of depending on my parents all the time, the way she used to. She and Lucy are more like equals. And talking with agency counselor. has probably helped her a lot, too."

This granddaughter and another who lived nearby stopped in occasionally for coffee and a chat, sometimes bringing one or two of their children. At least one of them took Inez shopping once each week and made certain she was driven to all family gatherings and festivities. Lucy, who had no children of her own, enjoyed the family visits almost as much as Inez did and was sometimes invited to family gatherings as well.

Living with her daughter as she had for more than 20 years from the time she was widowed, Inez was one of a declining minority. Sharing an adult child's home is not the housing arrangement of choice for most parents.

At a forum on retirement housing several years ago, participants stressed their strong desire not to be dependent on their children. One woman summed up the general consensus this way: "I have a very fine relationship with my children. I want to live near them, but not necessarily with them. My independence is as important to me as their independence is to them. I get a little help from them each month, but they get plenty from me in the form of loving and caring and a little babysitting."[1]

In fact, a study done several years ago showed that of the four out of every five persons over age 65 who had children, no more than 18 percent lived in the same household with a child. Another 55 percent, however, lived within 30 minutes of a child's home.[2]

Marie, who had been living in her daughter Josie's house for nine years, would have to be counted among that diminishing number who cling to the old ways.

"There was never any question about Momma coming to live with us after my father died. It's taken for granted in families like ours," said Josie, a trim, well-dressed woman in her early 50s, with dark eyes and a pleasant smile.

The same cultural expectations had dictated that Josie and her husband, a fruit and vegetable wholesaler, live with his widowed mother during the first ten years of their marriage.

"Sharing the house was a big help to us financially at the beginning. But when the children came, there was constant bickering over how to raise them. Then when Denny's mother had a stroke and I had to take care of her and three small children besides, it was very rough!"

After her mother-in-law died, Josie and her husband bought their own house in the same suburban neighborhood as her parents' home. Here they had their fourth child, and for a while Josie enjoyed the status of "queen of the castle," as she put it. When the last child started high school, Josie went to work as a secretary for a pharmaceutical firm, renewing skills she had practiced before the birth of her first child. Not long afterward, her father died.

Marie, a shorter, thinner, white-haired look-alike to her daughter and as well-groomed and carefully coifed, picked up the story. "After my Joe died, I sold our house and gave some of the money to Josie and Denny to buy this house. It's much bigger than their first house, and here I can have my own bedroom and bathroom—even when all the children are home," Marie said proudly, making certain it was understood that she had paid her own way.

In the same way, she spoke of how she cooked and baked and helped with the cleaning. Aside from deafness in one ear and a slight limp from an old hip injury, Marie seemed healthy, mentally alert, and energetic for such a slight 76-year-old woman. She praised Josie extravagantly, extolling her virtues as mother, housewife, and secretary to a "very important executive." She also spoke approvingly of her other two daughters, only complaining mildly of their living too far away and of the infrequency of their visits. No, she did not ever travel by herself and only visited them when Josie and Denny made the 300-mile trip and took her in the car.

Marie was also very proud of her nine grandchildren. "My Joe worked hard with his hands—a fine mason he was. But he only had a little education. Me, I went to high school, but I had to go to work before I could finish. But all my children went through high school and my oldest girl even took some college courses. Now, I think, all my grandchildren will go to college. It's wonderful to have such opportunities, and they're wonderful children," she beamed.

"I know Momma is quite happy living here," Josie said later. "She's the matriarch of the household. Even though I like to cook and bake too, I usually defer to her. And since I don't have much extra time, that's more of a help than a hindrance. The most annoying thing is that she follows me around the house all the time when I'm at home. And next is her interfering when we have problems with the kids. Lately that hasn't been so bad, partly because the kids are growing up and are away more than they're at home, and partly because Momma has some outside interests now, thank God."

The genesis of this last development occurred when Josie, worried about her mother's being alone in the house all day and isolated from people her own age, tried to persuade Marie to go to the municipal nutrition center for lunch. Marie resisted at first, saying, "You know what the neighbors will think when they see that van picking me up? They'll think I'm going to a soup kitchen because we don't have enough food in the house."

By introducing Marie to a neighbor's resident mother who attended the center, Josie finally convinced her mother to try it—first once a week, then gradually as a daily event. Finally, Marie even joined a seniors' club that met twice each week after lunch.

"It's just great!" Josie exclaimed. "Now Momma has a few friends to talk to and play cards with. And once in a while she'll go on a day trip with the club. It's made her less intense about the family and has taken some of the pressure off Denny and me."

Although she wistfully admitted that she sometimes felt uncomfortable in her own house, Josie thought that her minor discomforts were a small price to pay for her mother's well-being. "My mother's generation grew up with the idea that it was a disgrace not to be taken in by your children after being widowed. I haven't passed that on to my kids," Josie said. "And if it should happen to me, the last thing I'd want is to live with one of them."

Many of her counterparts in homes all across the country would undoubtedly agree, including Tamar, who lived in a town not far away. She and her husband had been sharing their home for the past four years with her 83-year-old mother, Olga.

A plain-looking woman of 60, neat in well-tailored clothing, Tamar had risen to chief community-relations officer of a large corporation after a little over two decades on the job. She was sober and intelligent, smiling rarely but with a smile that transformed her face. She and her husband, a utilities engineer, lived in a five-bedroom, three-bath, colonial house. Their three children having grown and departed, there was no scarcity of space. Olga had her own little suite of sitting room, bedroom, and bath.

When she was widowed 12 years earlier, Olga had sold her house and moved into an apartment in a two-family house in the same town, a few miles from Tamar's home. A plump woman with beautiful white hair that she tended faithfully, Olga had managed well until a series of small strokes resulted in memory lapses and speech difficulties.

"Mother's behavior became very erratic," Tamar explained. "She'd buy things she couldn't use and forget to buy necessities. And she was careless with her money. Trades people at the stores told me that she'd been giving money away—not waiting for change or leaving bills on the counter without picking up her packages. I think she realized it in her more lucid moments, because she asked me to take over her banking for her.

"Then I noticed that she'd stopped cooking and was subsisting on all sorts of junk food. I tried hard to get her to go to the town senior center, where I knew she'd get one good meal a day. I even went so far as to take time off from work to go with her. We tried a day-care program over at the hospital, too. But that didn't work either. She'd get all dressed up, and smiling and looking lovely, she'd sit on the sidelines—refusing to talk to anyone or to join them for lunch. When I asked her what her objections were, she told me, 'I'm surprised at you, dear. Those programs are for old people, not for me!'"

At her wits' end, Tamar offered to pay for a daytime companion for her mother, someone to help with the shopping, cooking, and cleaning. "For some reason, this angered her more than anything else. 'I don't need a nursemaid,' she said. My mother's a very sweet person. But she does have a stubborn streak," Tamar added.

After that, Tamar believed that her only recourse was to move Olga into her own home. "My two younger brothers live halfway across the country, so I was *it*," she said bitterly. "In some ways, of course, it's easier having her here than to be constantly traipsing over to her place to check on her and do all the chores. But she's alone all day here, too, puttering around, watching television, waiting eagerly—like a child—for John and I to come home. She's so dependent on us, we feel guilty if we go anywhere without her."

The worst part of the situation, according to Tamar, was that her mother became disoriented when they took her anywhere. Even on visits to her grandchildren, whom she loved dearly, Olga became confused and uncertain. "She's really gone downhill more quickly than I expected since she moved in with us," Tamar said sadly. "I often wonder whether she would have done better in a senior residence. With more social contacts and planned activities to stimulate her, maybe she'd have held on to reality a little longer."

It's difficult to speculate about the decline of one individual. Studies have shown, however, that the more control older people have over their lives, the more likely it is that they will continue to function well.[3] In a kind of see-saw effect, a fairly healthy ego is needed to maintain a good quality of life. But one of the troubles an aging parent may run into is keeping her ego intact as her lifetime roles slip away: the parental role shrinks as children grow; the career role fades with retirement; the spousal role dies with the spouse; even friendship roles diminish with the scattering and loss of friends. At the same time, the parent may have physical losses in coordination, hearing, or vision that can cause her to lose her driver's license, one of the main symbols of autonomy and mobility in our society.

If, at the very least, she can be mistress of her own home space, however small, it may help her to hang on to a modicum of ego. Sharing a home where the relationship fosters independence, as did Charlotte and Inez, is one way. For some elderly persons, it is better to have a separate living unit with its own kitchen, an accessory apartment, like Jenny's and Vera's. This is especially true for a parent sharing an adult child's home. Marie and Olga (and their daughters) might have benefited from more independent living arrangements.

One innovative way to allow elderly relatives to enjoy private but supportive living is ECHO housing. An elder cottage is a compact, free-standing, self-contained housing unit that can be set up adjacent to a single-family home. In Australia, where they are called "granny flats," more than 500 are in use. The Victoria Ministry of Housing installs and rents the cottages, which are moved from place to place as needed.

Efficiency units can be as small as 300 square feet, one- and two-bedroom units as large as 900 square feet. They are produced at the factory and can be finished in a variety of exterior designs to match that of the main house on the site. In most cases, one manufacturer says, the cottages can be put up in one day, including electrical, water, and sewer hook-ups, and can be disassembled in the same amount of time.[4]

In essence, ECHO housing is property sharing rather than house sharing, but it offers the same benefits—economy, independence, support, security, and companionship—with more privacy for elderly people and supportive families than any other sharing arrangement.

The drawback is that zoning codes and public attitudes have severely limited the use of ECHO housing in this country. Although the idea has been floating around for many years attracting wide attention and a few localities have passed permissive legislation, very few cottages have been installed so far.

A rural county in one eastern state has started a demonstration program with three elder cottages. Each cottage contains a bedroom, living room, dining area, kitchen, and bath; purchase price and installation costs total about $20,000. The county retains ownership of the cottages, and tenants pay a monthly rental fee that can be as low as $250. The rent is used to cover the cost of installation, insurance, and maintenance and to build a fund for the purchase of additional units in the future. When a cottage is no longer needed in one location, the county will move it to another.

Funding for the purchase of the first three units and to run the program came from state and federal housing programs. Income ceilings were set for occupants, who were limited to two people per cottage. At least one occupant had to be 60 years of age or older and related by blood, marriage, or adoption to at least one person living in the permanent residence. Other regulations specified that the owner must live on the property and set requirements on space and access to utility lines. Special-use permits were obtained from the municipalities where cottages were to be located.

Most applicants, according to the program director, were widows in their 70s, frail but still able to manage, who wanted to remain close or move closer to adult children. The children signaled their consent by registering as joint applicants.

Margaret, a 76-year-old widow with limited income and arthritic legs, was a typical candidate. For several years after her husband died, she rented the upstairs apartment in a two-family house. But the stairs became too difficult for her, and she had to leave, giving away or selling most of her furniture. After that, Margaret lived with her son's family in a small house in town for three months, then moved to her daughter's place outside of town for the next three months, before moving back with her son for another three months. She had signed up for an apartment in a senior housing project, but there was a waiting period of several years; in addition, the project was more than 30 miles from her home town and her family.

"The cottage has been a godsend," said Margaret's daughter, Bridget. "Ma's close enough so we can keep an eye on her. Yet she can putter around all on her own without getting underfoot in my house, which isn't very large, as you can see." Bridget and her husband were coapplicants for the cottage because their house stood on a one-acre lot, whereas her brother's house in town had little acreage around it.

"My mother is a simple woman," Bridget said. "She's never done any other job than being a housewife and a mother. She never even learned to drive. She's always depended on someone else for transport—first my dad, now me and my brother. Anyway, I can't tell you how much it means to have her nearby, safe and sound in my own back yard."

The cottage, about 20 feet behind the house, could not be seen from the front yard. A miniature house complete with white plastic siding and black asphalt roof, it resembled the main house but was much newer and brighter.

Margaret welcomed us inside cheerfully. The aroma of cinnamon and ginger filled the neat little house, so it was no surprise when our hostess, a woman of medium height, large girth, and hobbling movements, told us she had just baked some cookies and offered us a cup of tea.

The interior was much like a motel unit, with imitation wood paneling on the walls, sturdy carpeting on the floors, and ceilings made of pressed plastic. But Margaret's furnishings overcame the sterility of the basic decor. Handmade quilts, afghans, pillows, scarves, and doilies adorned the furniture, old but polished and clean. The small, convenient kitchen and bath had bright new appliances, easy to use and to clean, and such safety features as a grab bar on the wall next to the commode and a sit-down shelf on the molded shower wall. Doorways were wide enough to accommodate a wheelchair, should it be needed.

Margaret exuded pride and contentment. "I haven't ever had such new things, not anywhere I've lived. It's a dear little house, and I love taking care of it. And think how nice it is to have Bridget and Bob next door, and the children to drop in on their old granny when they're at home."

Both Bridget and Margaret spoke with admiration about how quickly the cottage had been set in place. "The truck brought it in one morning, and some workmen set it up on the foundation they'd put in a couple of weeks before. Then there was a lot of coming and going by electricians, plumbers, inspectors, who knows what all. By the next evening it was all hooked up and ready for Ma to move in. Incredible!"

Gazing out the window at an old apple tree in first bloom, the older woman murmured, "It's lovely. Just lovely."

In another corner of the same county, an 81-year-old widow, Frieda, had just moved into an elder cottage next to her grandson's house. The old house and the three acres around it had been part of the truck farm she and her husband had owned and worked during the 30 years of their marriage. After her husband's death, Frieda held onto the farm for 20 more years, trying to eke out a living with the help of her two sons, gradually selling off parcels of land until only the house and three acres remained.

"Neither of my boys wanted the house. They'd had their fill of farming. The younger one went down to Texas to work for an oil

company. My oldest rents a place in town and works down near the
city in some sort of defense plant. It's his son who owns the old
house," Frieda explained, pointing out the window.

She went on to tell how her grandson, Paul, had offered to buy
the house after his marriage about ten years before but insisted that
she continue to live there. "He's a good boy. Works in the same plant
his poppa does. And he tries to keep the house in good shape, too,
and puts in a big vegetable garden every spring. It makes me happy
to see it."

Frieda said she had stayed in the house for almost five years until
her grandson's third baby was born. "Oh, I love my darling great-
grandchildren, but the house was getting so crowded and noisy. And
I knew they needed my room for the new baby, bless him. So, it
was time to leave."

With the help of her family, Frieda found a second-floor apartment in an old house in town. The only access to the apartment,
however, was a long flight of metal stairs outside the house. "At first
I could climb the steps with only a little huffing and puffing. But as
time went on, it got harder and harder. Then I stopped going out
altogether unless one of the children came to help me. But I stuck it
out for five years. And I'd still be there if not for this little cottage."

Heart problems and diabetes made it necessary for Frieda to visit
the county health center at least once every three months. Since she
had given up driving the old farm truck when she was 72 ("The old
tank and I gave out at about the same time," she joked), either Paul's
wife or his mother drove Frieda to the health center; they also
shopped for her or took her shopping when she felt up to it.

A tall, once-sturdy woman now withered and bent, Frieda
leaned heavily on her cane when she walked. But her firm voice and
rugged face conveyed strength and determination. "I may be old and
worn, but I'm not yet ready for a nursing home. I never will be. I'd
have stayed in that apartment come hell or high water. But it would
have been lonely," she admitted.

"Here I can work in the yard, stop in and talk to the children,
look after the little ones. Often, they are over here. Once a week I
cook something special for the whole family, and we take it over to
the big house and have dinner together. It's good to be sharing this
place with the new generations." Frieda paused, then continued with
passion, "We old folks should pass on our property to our children,

but we shouldn't let ourselves be pushed out of the picture while we're still around. This is my home, too. I belong here."

A sense of belonging—to some place or some one; a sense of continuity—seeing the flow of life down through all the generations; a sense of worth—contributing in some way to the lives of others: these senses become more precious as we grow older. Any living arrangement that can contribute to their fortification is a winner.

Of course, tastes, needs, and means vary as much among the old as among the young, and no one living arrangement can be labeled best for all. What we have seen in this chapter is that housing that encourages the greatest degree of self-reliance seems the most desired and desirable.

Because of emotional ties and generational differences, bringing a parent to live in the same house with an adult child can make for a poor home-sharing arrangement; it often leads to irritations and conflicts within the home, sometimes spreading to siblings and other relatives. A separate apartment in a child's house may improve the situation, but much depends on the personalities involved. An elder cottage on the same property provides a separate domicile and increases the distance between the two dwellings, perhaps increasing the emotional distance as well by allowing greater privacy for the family and the parent.

Unfortunately, neighborhood attitudes and municipal restraints mitigate against separate dwellings. Accessory apartments are perceived as changing single-family zones into two-family zones and as lowering property values. And when the second dwelling is a visible, free-standing unit like an elder cottage, resistance is likely to be even greater.

One can hope that opposition to these housing options will change as the number of elderly people increases and the costs of housing and nursing-home care soar. Communities faced with shortages of affordable housing may come to realize that permitting accessory apartments is an excellent way to make productive use of unused space in many homes, in addition to extending a lifeline to desperate homeowners and home seekers of all ages.

The future of ECHO housing also may depend on bottom-line

monetary calculation. It costs about $50,000 to build a standard elderly housing unit, that is, a new apartment in a specially designed housing project. This compares with approximately $20,000 for an elder cottage, completely equipped and installed.

A prime supporter of ECHO housing, the American Association of Retired Persons (AARP) has mounted a campaign to educate the public about its economy and other benefits. AARP believes the concept can gain community acceptance by emphasizing that "neighborhoods will maintain their character and preserve their quality if local ECHO units are designed to: provide a temporary residence for relatives of the property owner; be removed from the site when they are no longer needed by the relative of the owner; and compliment the exterior of the original home."[5]

Anyone interested in elder-cottage or accessory-apartment housing for a parent or other close relative would do well to find out about local regulations and procedures. If there are prohibitions or unfair restrictions, you have a citizen's right to oppose them. Information and assistance are available from many sources (see the appendices for lists of resources). And once you start making inquiries, you may find more allies among your neighbors than you dreamed possible.

# 5

# Home, Sweet Home

*How to keep a house—including home-equity conversion and home sharing*

THE three women seated around the checkered-cloth-covered table talked animatedly. One of them had been away for two weeks, and the others were plying her with questions.

"Is your mom still in the hospital down there?"

"How's she doing?"

"Was she well enough for you to leave?"

"Who's looking after her?"

Polly held her hands up and said, "All in good time. I'll tell you the whole story, but let's order first."

Wednesday lunch was a ritual the three friends had followed for more than 30 years. Friends through high school, they had reunited after Polly returned from college and Marlene from a few years of working on the West Coast, settling in the vicinity of the small Midwestern city near where they had all grown up. Of the same age (near or just over 60) and similar backgrounds, they had shared over the years all the joys and sorrows of marriage, children, career decisions, family funerals, and weddings.

As they waited to be served, Polly began her account of her two-week stay in Florida. "The heart attack wasn't as serious as we thought, a 'minor episode' the doctors called it. But Mom being 90 now and so frail, they had to hospitalize her to be sure. She was home again after a week and would have been up to all her old tricks if I wasn't there to restrain her."

The other two remembered Polly's mother as a slim, attractive, energetic woman (very like Polly) who had worked in a city department store and later had become a buyer for the chain. Widowed at

60, she remarried a few years later and moved to southern Florida with her new husband. That was 27 years ago. When her second husband died, now 6 years ago, she had stayed on in their large, one-bedroom apartment overlooking the beach.

"I tried to talk her into coming back here with me, but she refused to hear of it. She loves the beach and ocean so. Even on days her arthritis flares up and she can't go out, she loves watching from the window. And she has her drama club and bridge group and—would you believe—a new gentleman friend," Polly chuckled.

"Your mom is a nine-day wonder!" Marlene exclaimed, a touch of envy in her voice. She had confessed her dislike for her own mother years before when they were schoolgirls, and over the years her aversion seemed to have deepened. As the three grew up and dropped the teenager's petulance toward parents, Marlene's attitude puzzled the others, especially Karen. "I can't understand why you feel that way. I always envied you. My house was such a mess, and yours was so neat and pretty. It seemed to me it would be lovely to have such a nice, clean, orderly home."

"The price was much too high. You wouldn't have liked it—your mother nagging all the time: 'Don't do this! Don't do that! Wipe your feet! Clean up at once!' She made my father's life miserable, too. A mean, selfish woman."

An only child, Marlene had adored her father, a kind, gentle man. But any show of affection between them, she claimed, had excited her mother's jealousy. When Marlene's father died at the age of 48, she blamed her mother. "The funny thing is I used to catch myself acting the same way with my kids, fussing about and tidying up after them, and feeling put out if Richard gave them too much attention," Marlene had once admitted about her own role as mother and wife.

Whereupon Polly had pointed out that this self-revelation should have increased Marlene's understanding of her mother. To which Marlene had responded, "I understand her better, but I feel she tainted me, and I still can't like or forgive her."

Marlene's mother at 81 still lived in the neat, pretty little house just outside the city where she had lived for almost 60 years, 43 as a widow. All about her, however, were deterioration and decay. The spread of urban blight to outlying areas of the city threatened to engulf the house. But the widow would not be moved. And Marlene, despite her hostility toward her mother, knew that something had to be done.

Karen had a similar problem. Her mother, also widowed and in her mid-80s, continued to live alone in an isolated, ramshackle farmhouse. Two older brothers had died, and only Karen and a younger brother remained; he lived in New York. In recent years, Karen, who had been divorced many years before, had considered moving back to the farm. But that would have meant a one and one-half hour drive each way to get to her job. Her friends dissuaded her, and she compromised by sleeping out at the farmhouse one night a week and over weekends.

"I don't really mind," she said. "There's something comforting about sleeping in my old bed, especially now that I've had the roof fixed and I don't have to worry about it falling in on me. I enjoy the quiet, the birds, all the country things after a week of hustle 'n' bustle. And Momma's always so glad to see me. She tells me a hundred times how nice it is to have me there."

Her friends wondered why Karen didn't persuade her mother to sell the old house and move to a city apartment near Karen. "Even if she agreed to do it, I think it'd kill her," Karen answered. "Remember, she was born in that house. It belonged to her parents. My daddy moved in when they married. She's always telling me, 'I was born in this house and I mean to die here.' But I do worry about her, living alone out there. Even though I call her every day and she can reach me, what'd happen if she fell or got sick and couldn't get to the phone?"

On this particular Wednesday, as the women talked over lunch about Polly's mother in Florida and rehashed some of Marlene's anxieties over her mother in a dangerous neighborhood and Karen's over her mother's rural isolation, Polly suddenly said, "Do you realize that we talk more about our mothers lately than we do about anything else!"

Back at her office, Polly was reminded of that observation when her secretary, Tricia, a woman in her mid-30s, asked for the following day off. "My grandmother's being released from the hospital. She's just over pneumonia, and she's still pretty weak. I'd like to get her settled down at home and meet the home health aides who are going to take care of her."

Polly knew that the younger woman had driven the 200-mile

round trip several evenings recently to see her 86-year-old grand-mother. She also knew that Tricia's mother had Alzheimer's disease and was being cared for by her father in their retirement home in Arizona and that the grandmother depended on Tricia as the closest relative. Separated from her husband and with a 6-year-old son, Tricia seemed near the breaking point.

When they talked again a few days later and Polly asked about the grandmother, Tricia wept. "Poor dear. It's taken a terrible toll on her. Her memory's been affected, and she's very frail and weak. I don't think she'll ever be the same again, and she knows it. The worst part is, she's terrified of being sent to a nursing home."

Fortunately, Tricia explained, her grandmother had enough money to pay for care at home, and she had given Tricia power of attorney. "What I've done is to hand the whole business over to a new agency here. The people who run it call themselves 'geriatric care managers.' They'll do anything from hiring a housekeeper to packing and moving an older person to a new place. A friend of mine who's a graduate social worker started the agency with two friends who were hospital geriatric case workers."

Tricia said they had arranged for a health-care service near her grandmother's home to supply round-the-clock aides for two weeks. The agency would maintain contact and evaluate the invalid's prog-ress during that time. Meanwhile, they had listed her grandmother's fine old brick house, which was in a respectable neighborhood, with a home-share matching agency in the area.

"Even when Granny's well enough to manage without the health aides, she's going to need someone there at night—if not for her sake then for mine," Tricia added. "I'm not sure how she'll feel about sharing her home. But it's certainly large enough. And I think I can persuade her that she needs a companion if she wants to continue living there."

The geriatric care managers would screen the home-share can-didates' applications and set up interviews for Tricia with those deemed suitable. She planned to introduce the person she approved to her grandmother. Tricia also counted on the agency to engage housekeeping help and to serve as liaison with the home-sharing agency, which would be monitoring the arrangement.

"If it works out the way I hope it will, it'll be a tremendous relief for me. I'll call Granny often, of course, and drive up with my little boy for a weekend once a month or so. And in the meantime I can try to get on with my life," Tricia finished with a sigh.

Polly, impressed by the pragmatism of the younger woman, asked for more details about the care managers. For, while Tricia was speaking, Polly realized how useful such services could be to her in the long-distance care of her mother in Florida. She was not mistaken.

On her first visit to the care managers, Polly described her mother's mental and physical condition and her surroundings. The picture that emerged was of an alert, well-groomed, 90-year-old woman with a heart condition and arthritis, still engaging in hobbies and personal relationships and interested in the world around her. Polly made it clear that her mother had lived in the same apartment in the same building for almost three decades, as had many of the other tenants. Though the building had not been specially designed for the elderly, many of its occupants, like her mother, had come from other parts of the country, were far from their families, and had grown old there. As a consequence, Polly thought, the older tenants had developed a close community feeling and a strong system of mutual aid and support, of which her mother was a part. Further, Polly said, she couldn't imagine her mother being happy anywhere else, thus moving her was out of the question.

What Polly hoped for was a part-time homemaker from a reputable agency to help her mother with shopping and household chores. The homemaker should also be someone Polly could count on to inform her quickly of any illness, as the neighbors probably would call only in case of a dire emergency.

A few days later, the care managers notified Polly that a homemaker had been hired for three days per week through a top-rated Florida agency. The homemaker would submit weekly reports to her agency to be transmitted to Polly by mail or, if the situation were more urgent, by phone. Bills were to be sent directly to Polly, as she had requested. The care managers charged a basic consultation fee and an hourly fee for the three hours of research, contact calls, and discussions.

Once the homemaking service was set up, the care-management agency withdrew; from then on Polly would deal directly with the

Florida agency. She felt the initial fees were worthwhile for the professional assistance provided and the time saved. And it was reassuring to know she could call on the care managers for additional services as needed in the future.

At their next Wednesday lunch, Polly told Marlene and Karen about the care managers. "They're like a surrogate family, but much smarter than most families. They can give you professional advice, and they've got a network of contacts with service agencies all over the state and the country."

Marlene was most interested and resolved to consult the agency about her mother. "Maybe they can figure out some way to help her. Every time I talk to her, we end up arguing."

The care managers' investigation of Marlene's mother, Mrs. K——, revealed that she had rejected all neighborhood outreach efforts to enroll her in community service programs like Meals-on-Wheels, senior-center attendance, or friendly visitors. She remained aloof, resisting any change or intrusion into the haven she had created within the walls of her house.

From the outside, however, the walls appeared literally to be tumbling down. Boards were rotting, and the front porch and steps sagged dangerously. Some of the storm windows had been removed; others were broken or warped and thick with grime. All in all, the house was scarcely distinguishable from its deteriorating neighbors on the street.

Mrs. K—— refused to allow the agency worker into her house at first, but after several telephone calls she reluctantly agreed to admit her. Inside, every article was clean and meticulously placed. Mrs. K—— proudly proclaimed that she spent most of her waking hours dusting, washing, and polishing in the downstairs rooms, where she lived. (The two upstairs bedrooms were closed off.) But the interior was sorely in need of paint and repairs: faucets dripped, ceiling and wall plaster flaked and crumbled, and linoleum and rugs were threadbare.

Mrs. K—— herself, a tall, bony woman, seemed weak and emaciated. Her steel-gray hair was pulled tightly back and coiled into a bun; her dress was neat, though spotted and mended; her shoes were worn at the toes and at the heels. She angrily asked whether Marlene had "foisted" the agency on her and insisted she could "manage quite well without any help, thank you."

After several visits, the agency worker was able to allay some of Mrs. K——'s suspicions. By appealing to her pride in her home, she convinced the older woman to apply to a nonprofit neighborhood housing committee that offered maintenance and repair services. Provided for elderly, handicapped, and low-income homeowners, services included carpentry, plumbing, masonry, winterization, roofing repairs, and window replacement. Most of the work was done free of charge or for a small fee, with funding from various sources, such as United Way, community-development block grants, state funds, neighborhood appeals, and foundation grants.[1]

Because of a long list of applicants, it would be at least six months before work was started on Mrs. K——'s house. And so far, she had given her approval only for exterior repairs. If Marlene wished it, the case worker would try to persuade Mrs. K—— to accept interior work as well.

The care managers also reported that the house had been registered with the neighborhood crime-watch group and was now on the regular patrol route. Mrs. K—— also had been listed with a church reassurance contact service that would telephone daily as a safety check.

Best of all, the agency worker had established enough trust with Mrs. K—— to take her shopping twice a week. (The first thing they did was to buy Mrs. K—— a new pair of shoes.) This had been one of Marlene's major headaches. She believed that her mother feared going out alone in the crime-ridden neighborhood and, consequently, curtailed her shopping until she reached the point of starvation. Marlene did bring in groceries periodically, but these face-to-face encounters were so unpleasant that she did so as infrequently as possible. She was happy to pay the agency worker for her time as a shopping companion and to confine her own filial duties to weekly phone calls.

"What a load off my mind!" she told Polly and Karen. "It's almost as if I'd found a long-lost sister to take over the care and coddling of Mother."

Even after all the years she had known Marlene, Karen could not fathom her friend's attitude toward her mother. Karen felt a great deal of affection for her own mother and was averse to having an agency take over tasks that she herself could do. She commented, "I don't think I want to spend money on an agency consultation. I've been doing some thinking, trying to decide how to improve my momma's situation. And I think maybe I've hit on a good way to do it."

A suggestion by a friend in the construction business had triggered Karen's idea to convert the upstairs of the farmhouse into a separate apartment. "More and more companies are putting up plants along the highway, and there's a big demand for housing out there already. We could rent the apartment to a young person or family, maybe lower the rent in exchange for them doing some chores around the house. Then it won't be so lonely out there for Momma," Karen told her friends.

A call to the county planning office established that there were no zoning restrictions in that rural location. But Karen was advised to get health-department approval of the well and septic system before starting the renovation.

Next, Karen discussed the idea with her mother, who had no objections, placing implicit faith in her daughter's judgment. When Karen warned her about the noise and dirt of construction, her mother was unconcerned. "I don't mind, Honey, because when it's over, we'll have something real fine. This house could use a lot of fixing!"

The big stumbling block was money. Karen had always found it difficult to accumulate any savings. After paying college costs for two of her children and investing in a few business ventures of the third, she had tried to start a new nest egg, only to deplete it on the desperately needed new roof for the farmhouse. Again, her friend in construction came to the rescue, informing her of a county housing coalition that offered deferred-payment loans to needy elderly homeowners.

Applying for the deferred-payment loan in her mother's name, Karen learned that it need not be paid back until the borrower died or sold the house, at which time the loan would have to be paid by the heir or by the proceeds from the sale. Since Karen knew she would inherit the house, she understood that she would be saddled with repayment of the loan at some future date. She wondered whether this was the best method for financing the renovation. To find out more, she consulted her lawyer, Polly's husband, Mac, and he reviewed several other home-equity conversion plans with Karen.

Mac first explained that these plans were designed to allow the homeowner to convert the asset represented by the home (the equity) into cash without forcing him or her to leave home. For example, he said, reverse mortgages of various types are long-term loans paid out in monthly installments to the borrower for a specified term, thereby creating a debt or mortgage that increases each month. The amount of the loan is based on a portion of the market value of the house, and that amount, plus interest and service charges, is due at the end of the contract, which can be from 5 to 15 years or until the owner dies or sells the property. In all likelihood, the home would have to be sold to settle the obligation. One of the major risks in time-limited reverse mortgages, in fact, is that the homeowner may outlive the term of the loan and be forced to sell the home to repay the loan.

A plan that guaranteed lifetime income payments would be best for people over 75, as Karen's mother was. But monthly payments would be very low in the case of the farmhouse, as its market value was low. The lower the value of the home, the less income can be drawn from it.

Karen rejected the idea of a reverse mortgage, first because her basic need was for a lump sum to improve the house, and then because she wanted to avoid losing the house. Mac agreed that it probably was unsuitable and added that, in any case, it was virtually impossible at that time to find institutions willing to negotiate reverse mortgages in most states.

Considering Karen's determination to hold on to the house, Mac thought a sale-leaseback arrangement might work well, particularly if Karen were the buyer. He told her how he had purchased his parents' home after his father had a stroke and needed the kind of home care his mother could not provide. As with most older people, the house was their primary asset. Its market value then was $112,000. Mac paid $15,000 down and obtained a mortgage for the rest, then drew up a rental agreement with his parents. He made a gift of the rent, however, so they paid nothing. With the money gained from the sale of the house, a single-premium annuity was purchased that paid the elderly couple about $1200 per month. They were also spared their former expenses of taxes, maintenance, and insurance, which Mac took over as owner of the house. This extra income enabled his parents to hire the home health aides they needed. The costs, together with mortgage interest and depreciation, became tax deductions for Mac. In addition, he boasted, the property was an excellent investment in a period of rising real-estate values.

Although the sale-leaseback appealed to Karen as a sure means of keeping the house, she knew she could not come up with the money for the downpayment. In addition, the monthly mortgage payments would be a strain on her budget while she continued living in the city. "I might be able to swing it after I retire and move out to the farm. But for now, it's not practical," she told Mac.

The one other possibility Mac mentioned was finding an investor or investment group to purchase the property on a sale-leaseback contract that would give Karen's mother (as owner) a lease for life. She would receive a downpayment and interest-bearing monthly installments on a note for the house. She would also have to pay rent. But the difference between the monthly payments and the rental fee would constitute extra income, to which could be added the money saved by the buyer's assumption of insurance, maintenance, and tax costs. Again, however, this plan jeopardized Karen's future ownership of the house. In addition, recent changes in tax laws may make this option less attractive to investors.

In the final analysis, both Karen and Mac agreed that a deferred-payment loan would best accomplish her aims. Though the loan would place a lien on the property, it would also result in improvement to the house and conversion of part of the space to produce income, thus increasing its value. And since the loan came from a nonprofit group and the interest was below the market rate, Karen felt she could manage the payments without undue hardship when she became the owner.

"It's going to be great," she told her friends after the loan request had been granted and the construction blueprints drawn. "You know how much I love that old place. Now Momma can have company out there. And in five or six years, when I retire, I'll move out there into a nice, new apartment." Then, in a dreamy voice, she added, "Maybe, when I'm as old as Momma, one of my children or grandchildren will come home to live with me."

Though we do not perceive it from day to day, life is fluid and constantly changing. When we observe someone for a while, as we have the "Wednesday friends," and then leave, we should remember that neither they nor their families can remain the same. Polly's mother, over 90 years old, may decline rapidly and need constant care. Should that happen, Polly will have some painful decisions to make. Should round-the-clock aides be hired? And could she rely on an agency to hire good people for three shifts? Who would pay for it? Should she, instead, move her mother? Into her own home or a nursing home? Near Polly and family or in Florida?

Marlene and Karen, too, will have to face new problems and decisions as their mothers age. But all three have learned a valuable lesson: There is help out there.

Public and private resources for helping the elderly to stay in their own homes are on the rise. Where government assistance has flagged, volunteer groups and private agencies are attempting to fill the gap. With the rapid growth of the older population, especially the 75-plus age group, many more such resources will be needed because, overwhelmingly, the living arrangement of choice for the oldest segments of the population is "home, sweet home."

In 1984, there were almost 18 million households headed by older persons. Of these, three out of four were owners; the others were renters. There were more male elderly householders who were owners (83 percent) than there were female householder/owners (67 percent). These figures are for noninstitutionalized people 65 years or older. Since only 5 percent lived in institutions, the majority of this country's 28 million elderly lived in their own or rented homes, and about one-third of them (8 million people) lived alone—6.4 million older women (41 percent of all older women) and 1.6 million older men (15 percent of older men). In fact, older persons living alone increased in number by 123 percent between 1964 and 1984, over two and one-half times the growth rate for the older population in general.[2]

This jump in the numbers of older people living alone is due to several factors, among them the greater population of elderly widows; societal norms that favor independence (general disapproval of living with children, for example); and improved economic security deriving from Social Security, Medicare, and government low-income assistance programs. For our purposes, it is enough to know that large numbers of older people—most of them women—live *alone* in their own homes. In addition, some of these women have incomes below the poverty level: of the 3.5 million elderly poor, three-quarters are women. And many, both owners and renters, live in homes built before 1940.[3]

Earlier in this chapter and in chapter 4, we discussed some ways to use the asset of a home to supplement income and to obtain companionship and services. If your mom is among those with limited income who are faced with the loss of a home unless they can come up with more money to pay expenses, one of the home-equity conversion plans could fit the bill. As we learned from Karen's investigation, each has its advantages and disadvantages, depending on the circumstances.

Basically, *home-equity conversion* is designed to help a house-rich, cash-poor homeowner unlock the value of a home and convert it into income without being forced to move or having to repay the loan from monthly income. The major types of plan are the *reverse mortgage*, the *sale-leaseback arrangement*, and the *deferred-payment loan*. In all these plans, home equity is converted to cash, either as a monthly payment or a lump sum.

The catch is that these plans are not widely available. Legal restrictions in some states discourage local lenders and investors; in addition, lenders are wary of making fixed-rate loans based on mortality risks, fearing that some older persons will outlive their home equity and that some heirs will contest the sale of the home to pay off the loan.

Home-equity conversion programs, capitalized by public funds, have been set up in a few states and cities; among them are California, Wisconsin, and Buffalo, New York. And a few private companies are venturing into the field. Consumer demand, however, has been low; either older homeowners are unaware of the existence of these programs or are unwilling to get involved in something so new.

A study by the U.S. Senate Special Committee on Aging reports: "Home equity conversion can be a complicated and confusing process. The concept is relatively new and it will be some time before sufficient experience is developed to provide national models and widespread knowledge of the process both among lenders and consumers."[4]

In the six years or so since this report was issued, interest in and experience with home-equity conversions have increased, and they may well prove viable alternatives for some older homeowners today. If your mother's major asset is her home and her income is low, it is certainly an area worth investigating. One important caveat: Seek expert legal and financial advice before your parent agrees to participate in any plan.

Such complex financial arrangements may be objectionable to older homeowners who see them as mortgaging the future and forfeiting their children's inheritance. Faced with income shortages, some may prefer renting out space in their homes. As we saw in our last chapter, the widow, Dorothy, and the couple, Rose and Tony, each converted a floor of their house to an accessory apartment to bring in extra income. (Karen also hoped to do this for her mother and even anticipated using the apartment in her own old age.) This served not only their needs, but those of their tenants, Jenny and Vera, as well.

Renting a room or two and sharing kitchen and other facilities in her home can benefit an older homeowner in the same ways: providing extra income, companionship, and the security of having another person available in case of accident or illness. Such was the arrangement of Lucy with Inez and of Martha with Charlotte. In the last case, Charlotte, the home sharer, provided services needed by the homeowner, Martha, in exchange for rent.

A disabled person who does not need extensive medical assistance can be helped to stay in her own home—whether a house or an apartment, provided it is large enough—by sharing it with others who will do chores and run errands. Often, a younger person or couple can be most useful. Sometimes close bonds are formed in home-sharing relationships: a younger person coming to be regarded as a child or grandchild by the older and vice versa, or a person close in age being regarded as a sibling.

Because privacy is so highly valued, however, many older people reject the idea of home sharing except as a last resort or as a preventive against institutionalization. Others do not have enough space to share. For these people, public and private agencies and programs stand ready to provide a multitude of in-home services: homemaking, health care, nutrition, telephone reassurance, friendly visitors, home repair, chore services, and many more.

For older people who do not need in-home services but are lonely and bored in retirement, volunteer opportunities are plentiful in most communities. ACTION, a federal agency, administers several volunteer programs through local grantees; among them are the Foster Grandparent Program (FGP), Senior Companion Program (SCP), and Retired Senior Volunteer Program (RSVP). The first two, FGP and SCP, offer low-income people age 60 and over the chance to work 20 hours per week for a small stipend, with expenses paid and the benefit of an annual physical exam. Trained and supervised by sponsoring agencies (schools, hospitals, day-care centers) foster grandparents serve four hours per day tending the needs of mentally and physically handicapped children. Volunteers in the Senior Companion Program assist homebound, chronically disabled elderly; indeed, delivery of many of the in-home services depends on these older volunteers.

RSVP, with no income limits on participants, serves a variety of organizations. Volunteer stations may include courts, schools, libraries, day-care centers, hospitals, Boy Scout and Girl Scout offices, economic-development agencies, and other community service centers. Volunteers may be reimbursed for transportation, meals, and other out-of-pocket expenses connected with their service. They receive a brief orientation from the local RSVP project director and in-service instruction after placement.

The retired executive who misses the old business milieu may be able to continue to participate through SCORE, Service Corps of Retired Executives, or ACE, Active Corps of Executives. These programs of the U.S. Small Business Administration link seasoned volunteer business people with owners and managers of small local businesses who seek management or technical counseling. The business pays nothing, nor does the consultant get paid, except for reimbursement of expenses.[5]

Earning money may be a more urgent matter than keeping busy or being of service. But finding a job is difficult for most older persons. To help provide employment opportunities for low-income people who are 55 and older, the U.S. Department of Labor subsidizes community service projects administered by public or nonprofit agencies or organizations. Projects must contribute to the general welfare of communities as well as increase the number of employment opportunities for older people. Some national contractors approved for funding are Green Thumb (an affiliate of the National Farmers Union), American Association of Retired Persons (AARP), National Council on the Aging, and the U.S. Forestry Service.[6]

Prospective volunteers will have no trouble finding eager takers, whether in the programs described here or in church or other community-based programs. Paid jobs are more difficult to come by, but it helps to know that there may be opportunities for your mom if she knows the right place to go. Those who do not want to or cannot work at a volunteer or any other job need not sit home alone either. Nearly every city neighborhood and every town has a senior center run by the municipality or county, by a community service organization or church group. Transportation is often provided, door-to-door or from some central location. Activities and programs range from card-playing through arts, crafts, and exercise classes to book discussions. Hot lunches (sometimes breakfasts, too) are usually served.

For many older people who live alone, the hours spent at a senior center constitute the focal point of each day, and the meal served may be the main source of nutrition. In some areas, meals are served at nutrition centers in schools, churches, or synagogues, and transportation is provided. Meals-on-Wheels programs are often run out of these centers; volunteers deliver a hot lunch and cold food for the evening meal, once a day, for the housebound elderly. Adult day-care programs also include meals in addition to providing health and other supportive services on an outpatient basis within a nursing home or other health-care facility.

For help with cleaning, laundry, cooking, shopping, and personal needs like bathing and dressing, you and your elderly parent can contact an agency for a homemaker. Many of the same agencies provide home health-care personnel. Regular home visits by registered nurses, licensed practical nurses, nursing assistants, home health aides, or therapists are usually obtained on the recommendation of a physician, often through a hospital social-service unit.

Fees vary, depending upon the agency and the services provided. If your mother's home health care is ordered by a physician, some of the costs may be eligible for reimbursement by Medicare and private health insurance. All persons age 65 and over are eligible for *Medicare*, the government insurance program that pays part of the elderly's medical and hospital costs through Social Security. Medicare will pay for skilled nursing care, but only after a hospital stay and only for three months. Neither Medicare nor private insurers will cover the cost of long-term home health care for chronic conditions. If your mother is in this situation and depletes all her personal savings, she may have to turn to Medicaid.

*Medicaid* is a health and hospital care assistance program for low-income people; it is financed by both state and federal governments and administered by each state. To find out about Medicaid eligibility and benefits, which vary from state to state, check with the social service or public assistance agency in the state where your mother resides. In 1985, 38 states offered Medicaid recipients benefits for home- and community-based services.[7]

In order to qualify for Medicare or Medicaid home health care reimbursement, your mother must use an agency certified by the U.S. Department of Health and Human Services; for Medicaid eligibility, the agency must also meet state requirements for patient care and financial management. An estimated 8,000 agencies provide some form of home care. For an additional check on an agency, you may want to contact the National League for Nursing and the American Public Health Association, which jointly accredit visiting nurse associations and home health-care agencies, or the National HomeCaring Council (see appendix IV for addresses).

When illness does strike, your mother will be inundated with medical bills and insurance forms. These can be confusing to someone in the best of health, so your help will be needed in sorting through them. If you have trouble, you can consult your local Social Security office (for Medicare information), the social-service department at the hospital, or a community legal-services organization. It may also be sensible at this time to suggest to your mother that she confer power of attorney on you or some other trusted member of the family to relieve her of the worry of financial matters.

In cases where the cost of medication becomes a hardship, substantial discounts are provided to income-eligible elderly by state pharmaceutical programs. Keeping a good record of prescribed medications is very important, especially for the person seeing more than one doctor, and it could be vital in the event of any adverse reaction. A pill container with compartments for days and times of day is a good memory assistant for the invalid who is alone; it also serves as a check on whether the pills were taken. A large calendar with clearly marked entries of medical appointments and other important dates is a wonderful addition to any household and is especially important for an older person.

But keeping those appointments can create problems. Unless your schedule permits you to accompany your mother, you should inquire about transportation and escort services to take her to and from medical appointments; many communities have such services.

A wide range of other useful home services, some of them crucial in enabling frail older people to continue living in their own homes, are offered through community and church organizations. Besides those already mentioned—meal deliveries, personal contact (visitor and telephone reassurance on a regular basis), home repair, legal and protective services—there are trained-companion services, volunteer chore and housekeeping services, barber and beautician services, and pastoral counseling visits by ministers, priests, and rabbis.

Innovative ideas cropping up in some areas of the country bring services like optometry and dentistry in mobile vans to the doorstep of the housebound. Recently a mobile clinic, staffed by retired doctors and nurses, began dispensing medical care to the elderly poor in Broward County, Florida.[8]

Parents with low incomes may need help from tenants' rights organizations, consumer advocates, and special utilities programs. Some cities and towns grant rent-raise exemptions to senior residents; some have tax-reduction or tax-deferment regulations that apply to elderly homeowners. In many areas, home energy-assistance programs help low-income households pay for their heat in winter and for heating-related emergencies, such as furnace repairs. Deductions on gas and electric bills and protection against utility shutoffs for nonpayment of bills, mandated by state laws, may also be applicable to your mother.

Utility companies are often a good source of information and assistance on energy-conservation measures for the home. They may give rebates on weatherizing and insulating materials or donate the material to low-income homeowners and apartment dwellers or to local home-repair agencies for installation; some will even do the installation for elderly or handicapped householders. Where life-sustaining equipment, like respirators and kidney-dialysis machines, are in use, the utility company should be notified. The company may be able to help with installation of emergency power equipment and also give the home priority for restoration of power during outages.

Telephone companies, too, have instituted programs for elderly householders: low-cost service and provisions for maintaining service when bills are overdue, usually by notifying a relative or friend who has agreed to be responsible. Blinking-light phones hooked up to teletype machines can also be installed for the hearing impaired.

It is a good idea to register your mother's name, if she has any functional disability, with the local fire department. Some fire and police departments collect information on residents of their community and store it in computer systems for use in case of emergency, and in-home alarm systems for the elderly and disabled are being used in some areas. The Life Safety System, for example, consists of home units that automatically alert the local fire department in case of fire or medical emergency. Home units are linked directly to the fire department by existing telephone lines and function in several ways: a no-activity alarm summons help if a subscriber does not check in within a predetermined period of time; a portable remote-control device can be used to activate a medical alarm; a monitor alarm in the home unit goes off at the firehouse if smoke and/or fire are detected. The fire department keeps a file on each subscriber that includes name, address, age, medical profile, and names, addresses, and phone numbers of physicians, relatives, and friends.

Developed as a cooperative public service by the International Association of Fire Fighters and the Muscular Dystrophy Association, Life Safety Systems, a nonprofit corporation, provides the equipment to interested communities at cost. Local fire departments usually base charges for installation of units on subscriber income. A few cities across the country are currently using the system to good effect. An excellent way to assure the safety of shut-ins and older persons living alone, its use is certain to spread.[9]

To find out about all the services available to the elderly calls for persistent sleuthing. The best place to start is probably your neighborhood church or synagogue. Religious organizations are traditional caregivers for the elderly and distressed. Often this work is done through a large, long-established community service organization

(Catholic Charities or Jewish Federated Services, for example), which may offer in its roster of services just what you are looking for. If not, you will probably get good advice on where to locate the information. Local senior, nutrition, and health centers are also clearinghouses for information on all kinds of programs for the elderly. Area offices on aging and social-service departments are good sources of information, too; but should you be disappointed, you may get better results by calling the state agencies. Local chapters and affiliates of national organizations like the American Association of Retired Persons and the American Health Care Association also can be helpful (see appendix IV for additional resources).

Those with neither the time nor the inclination to pursue the search can try to find a case-management agency to plan, locate, coordinate, and monitor services that will be professionally selected to meet your mother's needs. As yet this total approach—*geriatric case* (or *care*) *management*—is new. But with the bewildering profusion of programs and agencies in many communities and the geographic and/or emotional distance separating some parents from their children, geriatric care management promises to be a growing profession. Indeed, recognition of the need for coordination of the many community-based systems is creating a demand for local centers to assess the needs of older persons and arrange for home care, using a combination of public funds and private grants. Some public and private agencies, such as family case-work and mental-health centers, already provide a great deal of professional assessment and guidance for those unable to pay private-agency fees.[10]

No compilation of features that improve life for older people in their homes would be complete without mention of television and radio. Untold numbers of elderly rely on these electronic devices for information, entertainment, and companionship—albeit one sided. Their contribution to the quality of life for homebound individuals is incalculable. And whenever a TV set or radio breaks down, you can expect to receive an urgent call to remedy the situation.

For a visually impaired person, however, television may be frustrating. A fine substitute might be membership in the Library for the Blind and Physically Handicapped, part of the Library of Congress, which lends cassette tapes, records, and braille books free of charge. This service, started in 1934 with a wax record of Coleridge's "Rime of the Ancient Mariner," loaned out a total of 19,270,500 titles in 1984. Many of these books and recordings are enjoyed by older people, since it is estimated that more than half the people who are legally blind in the United States are over 65 years old.[11]

Of course, thousands of commercial tape recordings of books, plays, and music, not made specifically for the blind, can be bought in bookstores and in record and department stores or borrowed from libraries. And large-type editions of books, magazines, and newspapers, a boon to low-vision people who like to read, are also available in many libraries, bookstores, and by subscription.

Loss of hearing, another common problem among the aging, causes difficulties in communication and frequently leads to withdrawal from social contacts. In older persons, hearing impairment is often interpreted as mental decline. Yet some individuals refuse to acknowledge the loss, preferring to restrict themselves to solitary activities rather than risk the indignities associated with not hearing well. If your mother is among these people, persuade her to have an audiological examination. Advances in the field and technological improvements in hearing aids are helping many hearing-impaired people. And for those whose hearing loss is irremediable, some health centers run audio-rehabilitation classes and self-help groups.

What are some other ways to improve your mother's home life? What about the actual surroundings? Look around each room with an analytic eye. Even small changes can make a big difference in comfort and safety. Perhaps furniture needs to be rearranged to eliminate obstacles. Scatter rugs, loose tiles, or any other underfoot hazards should be removed and replaced with skid-free floor covering. In the bathroom, consider installing a grab bar, handrails, a seat in the tub or shower, and lever handles (easier on arthritic fingers) for faucets and instead of doorknobs. In the bedroom, are there a lamp and a telephone close to the bed? In the kitchen, are staples and essential daily utensils stowed in low drawers and cupboards? A whistling teakettle could be useful here, too. And don't forget a large, well-marked calendar, a clearly printed list of important numbers posted at the telephone, a compartmentalized pill holder, and any other simple memory-joggers that can help sustain a sense of self-confidence. (More details on household safety are given in chapter 7.)

Walking around your mother's home with her convenience and comfort in mind, you are certain to come up with many ideas of your own. Remember, however, that it is still *her* home. Except for unsafe conditions, you should change nothing without her approval.

Quite often your mom may be unsure about a change or say no when she means yes. The losses that come with old age do cause insecurity and uncertainty in some; others who have been negative types all their lives become more so. Even the insistence of some parents on remaining in their own homes may be suspect. Can you be certain that when your mother says, "There's no place like home, dear, no place like home!" she is actually firmly attached to her *present* home? Is living alone truly her preferred alternative? Would it be possible to change her mind if you were to explain and explore other options with her? Could she adjust to a new environment that improved on the old and eventually accept it enough to feel at home once more? You and other members of the family must make that judgment, but it is very difficult to walk the fine line between advising and assisting and taking charge of your mother's life. Psychological counseling and group discussions with people in similar situations may help. Later in this book, we offer some suggestions and guidelines. If and when you have concluded that your mother is genuinely determined to remain in her own home, you can make that home as pleasant, safe, and convenient as possible by using your own resources, those of the rest of the family, and those available in the community.

# 6

# Surveying the Field

*Comparisons of living arrangements*

I T may seem odd that we have not yet discussed retirement communities like Sun City, Arizona, and Leisure World, California, to name two of the larger ones. They are certainly highly visible, thanks to advertising, and probably form the background for the first image that comes to mind when one thinks of happy retirees—tanned, fit, and smiling as they bicycle along neat, sunny streets or swing their golf clubs on bright expanses of lush green fairways.

Where are the lonely, widowed, frail, and physically disabled older people? They are there, but often out of sight, in some of the older retirement communities. And that's exactly why we waited to introduce this living arrangement—because it is usually chosen by married couples at a time of life when they have adequate strength and income to pursue the active lifestyle to be found in retirement communities. Nevertheless, many a widowed mom has moved into one and enjoyed living there until an advanced age. So it is a viable alternative.

Other options we have not yet discussed are mobile-home parks, residential hotels, board-and-care homes, and foster homes. In this chapter, we describe these briefly and compare them with the living arrangements described in previous chapters and with the option of living with adult children.

To begin with, *retirement communities* (also known as *adult communities*) are complexes of permanent dwelling units for older adults. They range in size from as few as 100 units to as many as 45,000, with the average falling into the 4,000–5,000 range. Major areas of concentration in the United States are in Arizona, California, Florida, Texas, and New Jersey.

Almost always located far from town centers on tracts of unde-
veloped land available at low cost, large retirement centers (RCs)
become virtually self-contained towns. Most have community centers, clubhouses, and a variety of sport and recreational facilities;
some have their own shopping centers; a few may even have health-
care facilities. Larger RCs tend to provide a greater number and variety of services and more extensive recreational facilities and activities, and the more self-contained they become, the more likely they
are to be socially isolated from the population of the larger municipalities where they are located.

Minimum age requirements range from 48 to 55 and retirement
communities generally require at least one occupant of a housing unit
to be the minimum age and ban children under the age of 18 from
permanent residence.

A comfortable retirement income is needed to pay the purchase
price of a condominium unit and the monthly fees for recreation and
maintenance services. All communities provide some maintenance
service, although this varies widely: some provide service only on
the grounds, exterior repairs, and dwelling-unit upkeep; others provide water and sewage facilities, security police, street cleaning, interior repairs, painting, and so on. Bus or van transportation may
also be provided, but the automobile is still the favored way for getting around and getting away from time to time.

Essentially, retirement communities create a carefree, secure,
clean, well-ordered environment for friendly, outgoing, physically
active older adults who are in relatively good health—people who
feel they have "paid their dues" to family and society and now want
to enjoy life at play in the sun. Perhaps your parents are among the
lively retirees in one of these towns or villages. They moved there
in their 60s or early 70s and have found a good way of life, are safe
and secure, look after each other, and have made many new friends.

So it was with Karla and Philip. She was 65 and he was 68 when
they moved into a two-bedroom ranch house in Merryvale (not its
real name) near the mid-Atlantic shore. One reason for their choice
was the retirement village's proximity to a son, a daughter, and their
families, who lived within one hour's driving distance. Merryvale
was also only about 100 miles from their old city home and friends.
When surfeited with golf, painting, gardening, bridge, and partying,

they could hop in the car and visit their children or make the longer journey into the city.

"It was very pleasant—a happy time for both of us after all the years of hard work," Karla said with a sigh. "It seems a shame we had only six good years before Phil had his stroke."

Friends in the community were solicitous and helpful at first, Karla recalled. But after Philip returned from the hospital and during the two years Karla nursed him at home, they gradually drifted away, intent on their own pleasurable pursuits.

"I don't blame them really. Most people here don't want to think about illness and old age," Karla said. Explaining her own continued withdrawal in the year since Philip had died, she said, "So many social things are couple oriented, you don't feel comfortable if you're a single. And some of the wives get very bitchy if you even look at their husbands, as though you were out to steal her man."

Aside from some minor heart problems and mild arthritis, Karla was in good health. "But I feel so low, so drained of energy," she complained, "I can't seem to make any decisions. I think I should move, but I'm not at all sure—and I wouldn't know where to begin looking. I'm counting on my children to help me decide and to find another place if they think I should."

"It's ironic," she added bitterly, "but those who need the most support and friendship get the least in this kind of community. Most of us who are widows live behind closed doors."

Apparently the lifestyle that originally attracts a couple, with its heavy emphasis on recreation and an active social life, fosters friendships among couples. With the loss of a spouse, however, this coupling arrangement is severed, and the widow becomes the odd number at social gatherings. To avoid this, the widow must seek other forms of social contact or withdraw from socializing. While some make this transition successfully, those who were more dependent on their spouses end up feeling lonely and isolated. Of course, this often happens to widowed older people in other living arrangements, but it can be intensified in retirement communities because of the self-containment and active social surroundings, particularly if one once belonged and now feels rejected.[1]

On the other hand, some widows do make the transition with relative ease. For example, an 83-year-old widow in a large West

Coast retirement community spoke cheerfully of all her club and church activities. During her 20-year residence (the first 14 years with her husband), she had "formed long-term friendships and found a sense of community" that withstood her transition to widowhood. Others in the same community, though they complained about being in crowds of women so much of the time and about the superficiality of some of their friendships, kept busy and reasonably contented.[2]

Personality, age, and physical condition are at least as important as marital status in their effects on retirement-community living. Illness, disability, or a slowdown in physical activity due to advanced age limit social participation and may increase feelings of loneliness and isolation. Retirement communities, therefore, are not suitable living arrangements for the old and frail or even for the younger retirees who want their retirement move to be the last move they will have to make.

People in this last group, who are in the middle and upper income brackets and who are mobile and not chronically ill, may want to consider *congregate housing* (CH) or a *life-care community* (LCC) instead. These differ from retirement communities in size, location, average age of residents, and services offered. In contrast to the much larger RCs, congregate residences and LCCs average 150 units, with a maximum of about 350. And while RCs are usually located far from town centers, many CH residences and LCCs are located fairly close to or in towns. The latter are also more widely distributed throughout the country, rather than being concentrated in sunbelt states.

Minimum age for residence in CH and LCCs is 60 to 62 years, and the average age is in the low 80s; in RCs, the minimum age ranges from 48 to 52 years, and average age is in the high 60s to the low 70s, depending on how long the retirement community has been in existence.

While recreational services are offered in all three living arrangements, congregate housing and life-care communities also provide life-support services (meals, housekeeping, emergency medical care); in addition, LCCs provide complete health care, including long-term custodial nursing care if needed. For this reason, LCC residents need never make another move; CH residents may not have to either, but some RC residents will have to move to a more supportive environment later in life. (Chapter 3 also discusses congregate housing and life-care communities.)

Another of today's retirement options is the *mobile-home park*. The greatest concentration of such parks is in western and southern states, but they can be found throughout the country. Most mobile-home parks are not age specific, but some are age dense—housing large numbers of residents who are 60 and older. Owning or renting a mobile home is less expensive than buying a home in a retirement community or paying for congregate housing or for entry into a life-care community. Many parks have clubhouses, but group activities are usually generated and organized by the residents themselves.

In general, mobile-home parks are chosen by older people (usually couples) of moderate means who want a community lifestyle, but one that is more age integrated and less expensive than a retirement community. Good health and some stamina are requisites to this kind of lifestyle; if and when those go, another move may be necessary. As in a retirement community, widowhood in a mobile-home park may be isolating.

Some widows, dissatisfied with living alone in an apartment or house, choose to move into residential hotels. *Residential hotel* is a broad term used to cover a wide range of accommodations, from modest to luxurious. Those specifically designed for the elderly are called *retirement hotels*, some of which may have planned recreational and leisure activities. Furnished rooms, maid and linen service, and two or three meals a day are provided at costs that approximate congregate-housing fees. Most residential hotels are run as private, for-profit enterprises, whereas most congregate residences are under church-related, nonprofit ownership. Residential-hotel living, probably because it is less structured, is also less cohesive and less conducive to making friends and developing mutual aid and support systems than some of the other communal living arrangements.

For the older relative who is having difficulty coping with daily home chores and who needs more supervision than is given in other living arrangements, a *board-and-care home* may be the answer. Once a fixture in every town, in more recent times boarding homes have come to be used for the frail and for mentally and emotionally impaired patients released from institutions. They often shelter and care for people of mixed ages, many of whom have not lived in their own homes for a long time. Coming from dependent environments, boarding-home residents are less able to cope and require more supervision than congregate-housing or group-shared living residents.

In concept, board-and-care homes are similar to group-shared homes, but board-and-care homes are usually larger—25 to 30 residents—as compared with the 5 to 15 in most group-shared homes. Smaller size and less regulation in group-shared homes enable residents to have greater control over their own lives and create a better climate for formation of a substitute-family atmosphere.

A *foster home* is another possible alternative for the more dependent older person. It differs from a board-and-care home in that it is a single-family household with no more than four nonrelatives living in as paying residents. A good foster home will treat residents as family members, encouraging them to participate in normal family activities.

Board-and-care and foster homes are licensed and strictly regulated in many states. Their elderly residents often have little income, receiving only supplemental security income from the Social Security Administration, so there is little incentive to operate these types of homes. In order to keep them up to standards, some state governments have funding programs that offer assistance. Increasing shortages of affordable supportive housing for the elderly and the high cost of nursing-home care may engender more support for board-and-care and foster homes in the future.

Because discussions of types of housing alternatives for older Americans may create the impression that large numbers flock to them, a brief rundown of census figures should give us a truer perspective. In the 1980s, only about 15 percent of the nation's approximately 28 million people age 65 years and older lived in some form of planned housing specifically designated for the elderly (including subsidized housing projects, retirement communities, congregate housing, and life-care communities). Another 5 percent lived in institutions (nursing homes, hospices, and the like).[3]

Of those not in institutions, 2 percent lived with nonrelatives in house-sharing, group-shared, boarding, and foster homes. The majority, 67 percent, lived in some sort of family setting: three-fourths of the men with their spouses and about one-third of the women with their spouses. Thirty percent lived alone. (More women were alone or with nonrelatives than lived with spouses—43 percent and 38 percent, respectively.)[4]

These figures show that alternative living arrangements thus far accommodate only a small proportion of the elderly population and that traditional forms of housing still predominate. The factor that has changed most is the increased numbers who live alone—a 123 percent jump from 1964 to 1984. Among elderly widows, the percentage who live separately from relatives went from 28 percent in 1950 to 68 percent in 1979. Ten years ago, only 18 percent who had at least one child (four out of five older persons) lived in the same household with a child; that figure, too, may have decreased since then.[5]

Analysis of recent census data indicates that most elderly parents who move in with their children or other younger relatives do so for financial reasons. The second major reason is declining health. Another is the fear and anxiety triggered by the loss of a spouse. But it is almost always an act of last resort.

Most older people prefer living in their own homes but near family members. They understand the possible disadvantages of moving in with an adult child: loss of control over their life; the sense of becoming a guest in another person's home; loss of privacy, perhaps having to share a bedroom or a bathroom; conflicts and misunderstandings that may arise if they become overly involved in children's and grandchildren's lives. And if the child's home is distant from the parent's old home, it may be difficult to maintain old friendships and to find transportation and other services. Being dependent on family for transportation, companionship, and entertainment can lead to frustration and resentment on all sides.

Adult children who make room for parents in their homes also sacrifice some privacy and freedom. The child may have to tolerate interference by the parent in family and household matters, may lose some of the freedom to pursue work and leisure activities, and may even be treated like a small child again, undermining his or her authority and self-confidence.

Some of the disadvantages can be ameliorated by making use of community programs. Adult children can arrange for the parent to attend a senior center or adult day-care program to take some stress off the caregiving family; respite-care programs and companion services are helpful when the family wants or needs to get away from home for a while.

Counterbalancing the problems are some advantages. Living with an adult child is certainly the most economical living arrangement for the parent. It is also reassuring for the parent who needs care to be in the home of someone who cares about her; the parent feels loved and the child feels needed. The older person is often a rich source of advice and comfort to the family. And both parent and child may be rewarded by praise and increased status with friends and other family members, particularly in some ethnic groups.

If having mom move in with you appears to be a good solution to the question of where she can live, a separate apartment in your home or a cottage adjacent to it may serve as a safeguard against loss of privacy and the frayed nerves brought on by too much togetherness. In the case of an overly demanding parent or one who needs a great deal of care, however, just being in close proximity can put a strain on the relationship. And after all is said and done, it is this precious relationship that can become the worst casualty of living with mother.

For most older people who can no longer live alone in their own homes for whatever reason (except those with serious disabilities that call for nursing care), age-specific communal living has many advantages over living with children. By *communal living*, we mean specially designed subsidized housing projects, congregate and life-care communities, residential hotels, board-and-care and foster homes, and home sharing—group or single. We do not include retirement communities and mobile-home parks, where living alone is essentially the same as living alone in a home anywhere else.

As opposed to living with children, communal living gives an older person some breathing space and independence from children. It also gives her more control over her own life and more opportunity to interact with her peers, to form friendships, and to engage in leisure and hobby activities. By providing some or all of the support services that may be needed, communal living arrangements relieve the pressure on children who may previously have been the sole providers. Indeed, numerous studies have shown that living in communal types of housing often improves relations between children and the parents who formerly lived with them or who lived alone and relied heavily on them for assistance.

Communal living, though more expensive than living with children, can be less expensive than living alone. It is also more supportive, fostering friendships and mutual aid and support among peers, offering needed services when and if necessary, and ensuring help in case of emergency. The last is especially important in that it eliminates the nightmare anxiety of both the elderly parent living alone and the child: the image of mom lying helpless somewhere in her home, injured or ill and unable to get to the telephone. Studies of communal living—particularly subsidized housing, congregate housing, and life-care communities—indicate that residents live longer, healthier, happier lives and spend less or no time in institutions when compared with their peers who live alone in ordinary housing.[6]

If your mother lives with you or alone and wants to make a change, what will she need in the way of financial resources? And how available are these communal living options we have been discussing? Finally, how do they compare with each other with respect to their impact on the emotional and physical well-being of older people?

Financial requirements vary widely. Life-care communities require the highest level of income and assets, a middle or upper income; congregate housing and group-shared homes require moderate to middle income; subsidized housing (which may include some group-shared, boarding, and foster homes) require low to moderate income. Residential hotels range in cost from moderate to high. And home-sharing can involve people of any income level, depending on the specific arrangement.

On the question of availability, subsidized housing, mostly in the form of apartments, constitutes the largest segment of communal housing for the elderly in the United States. By 1982, this amounted to over 1 million units in projects ranging in size from fewer than 10 units to over 900 units and from high-rise towers to low-rise garden apartments and individual units scattered on individual sites. Unfortunately, there are long waiting lists for this type of housing. Though accurate figures are not available, it is estimated that at least as many elderly are waiting for federally subsidized housing units as currently occupy them.[7]

To qualify for an apartment, an applicant's income and assets may not exceed a certain level, and she must be able to function independently. Because federal programs for building new projects have come to a virtual standstill, state housing finance agencies are strapped for funds, and very little new housing of this type is being built at present. Its future is equally uncertain.

Life-care communities and congregate housing are next most numerous in this country. But waiting lists can be as long as eight to ten years here, too. Applicants must have the financial means for entry fees (for LCCs) and monthly payments, and they must be mobile and able to care for themselves.

Some states, like New York, prohibit life-care communities in order to protect consumers against financially unsound operations. "Because health-care expenses and turnover rates are impossible to predict accurately, some life-care communities have encountered difficulty in meeting expenses while fulfilling the obligations of their contracts," one investigator explained.[8] Most states, however, rely on regulations and standards to eliminate unscrupulous operators. In addition, the American Association of Homes for the Aging has established the Continuing Care Accreditation Commission to review and evaluate LCCs according to a set of published standards (see appendix II for address).

LCCs and CH are being built at an accelerating rate by both nonprofit and for-profit organizations, most without subsidies. This trend is likely to continue because developers are attracted by the large potential market—growing numbers of elderly who are in need of a more service-supported environment and who can afford to pay for it. The market has been swelled, too, by changing attitudes about living with children among the generation now coming into old age and by changing family life that has reduced the numbers of traditional caregivers, as the daughters are now immersed in careers of their own.

Formalized group-shared homes are fairly recent housing arrangements for the elderly. This is also true of home sharing.

Though done informally throughout modern times, what is new now is the part played by service agencies in matching homeowners and home sharers to help expedite and improve the arrangements. By 1982, more than 200 housemate matching services were in operation in metropolitan areas across the nation.[9] Without agency help, older owners would be naturally reluctant to interview strangers in their homes, and seekers would be fearful of entering the homes of strangers.

Although still not widespread, there has been a spurt of group home sharing in recent years. This is likely to continue, mainly because large sums of money are not needed to initiate and develop group-shared homes; community groups can undertake a shared-home project using local energy and expertise without depending on government assistance.

Indeed, a group of individuals can plan and develop its own group-shared home. One such group of eight women has a plan to form "a community to be together when they are old. The women knew each other in school and decided that they didn't want to have to rely on children and government systems to take care of them in their older years. . . . Each contributes $200 a year. This money is invested and held in trust. They meet together once a year and have a commitment to help each other when they are old."[10] Multi-generational group-shared homes also can be found in a few communities, such as Boston and Philadelphia.

Perhaps because the concept is so new, there are usually no waiting lists for group-shared homes. Income limits are rarely set either, and some functional disabilities are acceptable as long as residents can care for their own personal needs (dressing, bathing, and so on). A sponsoring organization may, however, attempt to match residents in order to encourage a stronger feeling of family.

*Elder Cottage Housing Opportunity*, or *ECHO housing* (a cottage adjacent to a main house), is practically nonexistent in this country, though it is being used widely and successfully in Great Britain and Australia. Small programs in Pennsylvania and California and a demonstration program in western New Jersey may help spread the idea, but zoning laws are a major impediment. A few states have adopted laws permitting ECHO housing, but most local jurisdictions have not yet accepted it. This type of living arrangement need not pose any income or physical limitations on the cottage tenant. And if local laws were to allow it, a cottage could be erected on an individual basis by a property owner.

Among the benefits of communal living, as we mentioned earlier, are the greater opportunities for social interaction, friendship, mutual aid and support, security, and activity. These benefits are often accompanied by a reduction of pressure on and demand for services from adult children and by improved intergenerational relations. These may be called quality-of-life factors. How do the living arrangements we have been discussing compare with each other in this respect?

When we break it down, we find that a life-care community offers the most support and enables the resident to spend the rest of her life there, no matter how old, frail, or disabled she may become. She can live independently in her own private unit as long as she is able and still be assured of various levels of care as her needs change. Therefore, she need never make another move. Of course, she must be able to afford the high cost of entry and monthly fees, and she must move into the LCC while still functioning relatively well.

Congregate housing is the next most supportive kind of housing and is similar to an LCC in all things except the guarantee of continuous lifetime care. Therefore, a CH resident whose needs change will have to move.

In a subsidized housing project, elderly residents have the support of their neighbors, but little more. When older, frailer, and less mobile, they will need services from family and community in order to stay in place. Congregate services such as household help and meals can prolong tenancy, but they are available in only a few regions of the country. As with congregate housing, a serious deterioration in a resident's condition mandates a move to an adult child's home or to a health-related facility.

Group-shared homes offer support services similar to those in congregate housing, but more economically and on a smaller, more informal scale. At the same time, the group-sharing resident must settle for less privacy than someone living in an LCC, CH, or subsidized project apartment. She will share kitchen, living, and dining rooms and probably a bathroom as well. Common living areas also mean she will have less control over her life—what and when she eats (also true of LCC and CH for at least one meal per day), who and how she entertains, even what chair she occupies in the living room. A good arrangement, however, encourages input by residents on meal planning and use of common rooms. In any case, group-shared housing demands cooperation and skill in the art of compromise.

Another difference between group-shared homes and other living arrangements is that there are fewer people with whom to socialize and develop friendships. But, for the same reason, the possibilities for developing a sense of family are greater. For the person who might have difficulty adjusting to large numbers of people, living with a smaller group will seem less threatening and more like living in a home of her own with an extended family.

Home sharing involves a loss of privacy similar to that of group-shared homes, but the loss of privacy involves only one or two other people. Having so few others to interact with may be an advantage or a disadvantage, depending on the personality of the home sharer. The supportive nature of this kind of arrangement is limited to the possible companionship and security of having another person in the house and to whatever services were agreed to be exchanged when the sharing agreement was made. Any future physical decline will necessitate a move to a more supportive environment, as in all the other living arrangements except for the LCC. While it lasts, a home-sharing arrangement enables the elderly homeowner to stay in her home and the sharer to have the nearest thing to being in her own home.

It always comes back to that—the nearest thing to being at home. For most people, emotional ties to home become stronger as they grow older. People over the age of 65 move far less often than younger people, and the majority of them move to another residence in the same state. In recent years, however, the numbers of older people who moved have increased; and the numbers who moved from one state to another increased by 50 percent in a decade, as compared with the previous decade. Nearly half of these older migrants went to live in the sunbelt states. For the most part, they were relatively affluent, well educated, and moved with a spouse.[11]

Among them were Lois and Ed, both in their early 70s. She had been an elementary-school teacher; he had run the small-town (New England) family clothing store inherited from his father. After a heart attack, Ed had sold the store, he and Lois had sold their house, and they moved to a pleasant condominium in a high-rise building on the Gulf coast of Florida. One daughter, Alice, lived in western New York State, where she taught high-school science.

Alice had been married twice: the first marriage ended in divorce, the second with the death of her husband several years before her parents moved south. Three stepchildren and five of her own and her teaching job kept her totally occupied. She had a loving relationship with her parents but was unable to help them with their move or to see them very often. She kept in touch by telephone.

"My dad died three years after they moved," Alice continued the story. "Mom was a wreck for a while, but she stayed on in the Florida place for another five years. By that time she was 81, still very energetic—walked a lot, active in several senior clubs, and generally kept very busy. But a fall and a broken hip laid her up for a long time. I made several rush trips down there, and when it was time for her to leave the hospital, I arranged to have round-the clock practical nurses look after her at home."

After her recovery, Lois came north to live with her daughter. "It wasn't bad for me," Alice recalled. "I've always spent very little time at home. When I did get home at night, it was kind of nice having Mom there. But she didn't like it. She was lonesome and bored, with no one to talk to all day. And the business of meals was a pain. I'm used to eating dinner out, so I'd leave something for Mom to warm up for herself. But she never bothered—said she didn't like eating by herself. After a while, I felt compelled to come home and prepare dinner every night."

Nevertheless, Alice said, she was willing to continue the arrangement. But before the year was out, Lois was "itching to leave." The problem was, Where could she go? "We both knew she'd be as lonesome, or more so, in her own apartment. So we called the county agency for the aging and got a list of retirement places, visited the ones closest to my apartment, and settled on a small, 56-resident hotel about 12 miles from here," Alice explained.

That was four years before. Seeing Lois, who was then 86 years old, in the lounge area at the hotel corroborated Alice's description of her as "doing just fine." Trim, attractive, well dressed, her white hair short and haloed around a remarkably unlined face, Lois kissed Alice and greeted the rest of us warmly. At her suggestion, we walked out to the back garden. Lois, using a cane, managed to walk briskly despite the limp from her old hip injury.

The hotel, about a block away from an unused railroad depot, had a faded grandeur about it—like many of its residents. Four stories tall, about a half-block wide, and on the edge of the town's commercial district, the masonry building was ornamented with fancy cornices and lintels. Inside were large, wood-paneled common rooms and large, high-ceilinged bedrooms with walls papered in old-fashioned patterns above the wooden wainscoting.

"I like it here," Lois said. "The building is about the same age as I am, and it reminds me of some of the old buildings in my home town. I can close my door and be alone in my room, or I can have plenty of company. I've made a few friends. We play cards together or walk to the shops, the hairdressers, or the bank. Sometimes we take a bus to one of the theaters or the library. I hope I stay well enough to live here for a long time."

Later Alice remarked, "That's the big 'if.' How long will she be able to live there? We both would have preferred a life-care community. But we wanted to be near each other, and there don't seem to be any life-care places in this area."

Alice introduced us to a friend whose mother followed a reverse pattern: the mother, Bettina, left a congregate residence in the South to come and live with her son, Fred, and his wife, Penny. After the death of his stepfather, Fred was determined to bring his mother into his family fold. "I honestly believe that a family should be as close as possible. I think my mother needs us, and we need her," he declared. He and Penny fixed up a small suite—bedroom, sitting room, and bath—for her. Bettina was 89 and Fred, her only child, was 68 when he prevailed upon her to come home with him. And so Bettina, still unhappy over the loss of her husband three years earlier and little caring where she lived, moved north.

Almost at once, little problems began to crop up. Fred and Penny, who both worked out of offices in their home, Fred as an investment-fund manager and Penny as a freelance writer, were interrupted frequently by Bettina seeking company. They realized that she was lonely and introduced her to their small town's senior group. The group met only once a week, however, and were all old friends. Though they welcomed Bettina, she felt like an outsider. She continued to rely on Fred and Penny for companionship.

Another consequence the couple had not foreseen was the impossibility of leaving Bettina alone at home while they went off on a trip, as they were used to doing. "I wasn't going to let that stump me either," Fred exclaimed. "We hired a companion. Ginger is here from 9 to 5 on Monday through Friday. And when we go on a trip, we arrange for her to stay as long as we're gone. It's true we can't afford to go on as many trips now," he added with a laugh. "But I think it's worth it to have Mother with us."

Bettina, a tiny, fragile, wrinkled woman, impeccably dressed, was less certain: "I don't know if I can be happy anywhere now that my husband's gone. I only know I hate getting old. In the congregate residence there were lots of others like me, which had its good points and its bad points. Here, I know I'm loved and will always be looked after. And now that Ginger is with us, it's not quite as lonely."

Lois and Bettina are just two examples of what demographers are calling *countermigrants*, those people who moved to the sunbelt at retirement and are now returning to their home states or to their children's home states. Countermigration, though it involves relatively small numbers, is considered a significant trend.[12]

With increased longevity, more—and more frequent—changes in geographic distribution of the elderly can be expected. And the longer we humans live, the more likely we are to make at least one, and perhaps several, changes in our living arrangements during our later years, just as Lois and Bettina did. That is why gathering all the information we can on housing options for older people is so important.

# 7

# What's Your Pleasure? And How to Find It

*Guidelines for helping your parent make housing decisions*

Now that you have an idea of some of today's housing options for the elderly, it's time to sit down with your mother to discuss her feelings and expectations.

It may not be easy. Many older folks (as well as some younger ones) are fearful of change. The very thought of leaving familiar surroundings can be upsetting to an older person. But as long as your mother is fully competent, it's important that she make the final decision. Her assent is crucial to the success of any move she might make.

Your role should be to inform, advise, and assist your parent, a sometimes difficult role for a child to assume. It means admitting to yourself that your mother is growing old and persuading her to acknowledge it herself. Don't be put off. The objective is worth the effort:

It can happen that your mother and father may view your efforts at a partnership with distrust and resentment. They may rebuff any seeming intrusion into their private lives. But they are just as likely to respond positively—respecting, even welcoming your opinions—although even the most receptive may not be ready to start planning at the same time you are. It may take them more time, but eventually they may be willing to share the planning process with you or take it over themselves. If not—if all attempts fail and you make no progress at all—you will at least have the small comfort of knowing that you have thought through some plans of your own and will therefore be better prepared yourself to know what has to be done if the day ever comes when they cannot manage on their own.[1]

When your parent is ready to talk about her future, a look at her present housing situation, lifestyle preferences, financial resources, health, and functional ability can shed light on what direction your joint planning should take. Answering the following questions should provide an objective basis for your parent's decision on whether she ought to stay, whether changes are needed in her present living arrangement, or whether a move might be best. The questions are framed for your parent to answer. No grades or ratings are given, since there is nothing absolute about them. Indeed, you may come up with some additional questions of your own. The answers are intended simply to serve as guides.

| *A. Home and Neighborhood* | *Yes* | *No* |
| --- | --- | --- |

1. Do I like my home?
2. Is it comfortable and pleasant?
3. Is it the right size? (Not too large?)
4. Is the neighborhood safe and attractive?
5. Is there good crime control?
6. Is it convenient to stores, banks, etc.?
7. Is it convenient to health and community services and facilities?
8. Can I get to my church or synagogue?
9. Can I get to recreational, cultural, and educational facilities (community and senior centers, "Y" buildings, theaters, colleges, etc.)?
10. Am I near family and friends?
11. Do I have someone in my house, apartment building, or close by in case of emergency?
12. Am I near volunteer and employment opportunities?
13. Are there opportunities for making new friends when old friends leave?

| A. Home and Neighborhood (continued) | Yes | No |
|---|---|---|

14. Are there opportunities for new recreational and hobby pursuits?

15. Does my present location allow me to get enough exercise?

16. Do I like the climate?

17. Is the climate good for my health?

18. Is it important to me to remain in the area?

| B. Physical and Financial Questions (Present and Future) | Yes | No |
|---|---|---|

1. Is my home safe and hazard free?

2. Does the physical layout match my functional ability? (e.g., Can I manage stairs? Reach cabinets and shelves?)

3. Is my home easy to maintain? Can I take care of it now?

4. Will I be able to take care of it for the next five to ten years?

5. Does my present home cost less than 30 percent of my income (including utilities)?

6. Will I be able to afford my home over the next five to ten years?

7. Will my home continue to be suitable even if my health or my mobility changes?

8. Do I own and drive a car?

9. Can I continue driving over the next five to ten years?

10. Is there public transportation nearby?

| C. Personal Feelings | Yes | No |
|---|---|---|

1. Do I feel content and not lonely or isolated in my home?

## C. Personal Feelings (continued)

| | Yes | No |
|---|---|---|

2. Do I have pleasant feelings and memories associated with my present home?

3. Do I find it difficult to make changes?

4. Do I prefer the familiar rather than new experiences?

5. Is it difficult for me to adjust to new friends and new social situations?

6. Is it difficult for me to meet new challenges?

7. Is privacy very important to me?

8. Is being independent very important to me?

If the answers to most of the above questions are yes, your parent is quite satisfied with his or her present living arrangement and plainly wishes to stay with it. The best that you can do then is to help make any changes needed for his or her home to be as safe and hazard free as possible, particularly if he or she answered no to questions 1 and 2 in list B.

According to the National Safety Council, the elderly have almost 30,000 fatal accidents in their own homes every year. Another 800,000 suffer severe injuries from falls and are disabled. And their hospital stays are longer than hospital stays for cancer and for cardiovascular and respiratory diseases.[2]

For improved safety in the home, we suggest you reread chapter 5 in this book, and we offer the following recommendations, adapted from *Safety for Older Consumers: Home Safety Checklist* (published by U.S. Consumer Products Commission, Washington, DC 20207, June 1986):

### Housewide

*Electrical*

• Check all wiring and plugs for fraying and other damage.

• Keep wires out of traffic flow to prevent tripping.

• Try not to use extension cords.

• Do not place furniture or rugs over wiring.

- Raise electrical outlets 18 to 24 inches off the floor.
- Make sure all areas are well lit.

*Floors*
- Make sure all rugs and carpets are slip resistant.
- Check for surface irregularities—broken tiles, loose boards, etc.— and eliminate.
- Remove raised doorway sills wherever possible.
- Avoid coating floors with slippery substances.

*Security*
- Locate and test smoke detectors.
- Review fire exit procedures.
- Check doors and windows for ease of opening and closing.
- Install locks where needed.

### In the Kitchen

- Be sure stove and ventilation system are in good order.
- Keep paper and cloth away from the stove, including loose-fitting clothing.
- Have sufficient light over work areas.
- Use lower shelves to store everyday dishes and utensils.
- Use a stable step stool, preferably with a hand rail, to reach higher shelves.

### In the Bedroom

- Keep a nightlight in the room or in an adjacent hallway or room.
- Have a lamp or wall switch within reach of the bed.
- Install an extension phone next to the bed.
- Keep a flashlight handy in case of power outages. Check batteries periodically!
- Keep any potential fire hazards (ashtrays, hot plates, heaters) far away from bedding. (Burns and mattress-related fires are leading causes of accidental death among older people.)

### In the Bathroom

• Provide nonskid floors in tub or shower.

• Attach securely at least one grab bar (two, if possible) to the wall of the tub. Or use specially designed bars that grip the edge of the tub.

• Place a small plastic seat with a nonslip bottom in the tub or shower. (A convenient device when taking sitdown showers is a European-type shower head that can be clamped to the wall or hand held.)

• Remember: shower stalls are safer than tubs because of the potential for a fall when stepping over the rim of the tub—even with grab bars.

• Attach grab bars to the wall or walls alongside the toilet commode. Or use a free-standing set of grab bars that fit around the commode.

### Halls and Stairs

• Be sure these areas are well lit with light bulbs of sufficient wattage. (Frosted bulbs reduce glare.)

• Install light switches at the top and bottom of the stairwell.

• Build sturdy handrails on both sides of the staircase.

• Check stair carpeting for tight fit and for rips or tears.

For the elderly parent living alone, particularly one at risk medically, a security alarm system can be a great comfort. These systems enable a person at home to summon help in an emergency. One such system, the Life Safety System (described in chapter 5), works at the press of an emergency button, which sounds an alarm at the local fire department. Other medical-alert devices are operated through local hospitals. A home transmitter signals the hospital operator when a button on a wristband or pendant is pressed. These devices have recently been improved to allow voice communication with the operator as long as the victim is within 50 feet of the telephone.[3]

A carrier-alert program sponsored by the U.S. Postal Service monitors individuals who sign up for the service; the mailman checks each day to see if the previous day's mail has been removed from the box. In addition, volunteer organizations in many communities maintain telephone reassurance contact with elderly people registered with them.

Following the above suggestions should help to make your mother's life at home reasonably safe and comfortable. But what if the majority of her answers to our questions were yes, but she answered no to A.3, A.10, A.11, B.5, B.6, B.7, C.1, and C.3?

This would indicate that she feels lonely and far from family and friends, in a house that is too large and that she has doubts about being able to maintain and pay for in the coming years. Add her admission of aversion to change, and you have a combination that calls for consideration of a home-sharing arrangement. Depending on the exact circumstances, you can safely advise your mom to rent out one of the rooms in her house (or apartment), share her home (with use of kitchen and other living areas), or create an accessory apartment (see chapters 4 and 5).

The person who answered yes to most of our questions but no to questions B.1, B.2, B.5, B.6, and C.3 should consider some form of home-equity conversion (described in chapter 5). Receipt of additional income will relieve the high housing cost and provide funds for proper maintenance and repair. Perhaps by means of a reverse mortgage or deferred loan, your parent can remain in her own home (as her response also indicates that she does not like to make changes) and still surmount some of the problems with her house.

You and your mother may judge from her response to the questions that her present living arrangement is suitable and preferred. But you ought to urge her to attend a community facility—a senior center, "Y" center, nutrition site, or adult day-care program—or join a volunteer work program, if she has not already done so. This is particularly important for those who said no to questions A.10 (Near family and friends?) and C.1 (Content and not lonely?).

Obviously, the older person who answered no to most of the questions is in need of a plan for a new living arrangement. And the more negative answers, the more urgent the need for some form of communal living arrangement. At the same time, if she said yes to most of the questions in section C (personal feelings), you can anticipate your parent's difficulty in accepting a move.

Even the person willing to go through the moving process may not be able to overcome the ingrained belief that communal housing is also institutional and means loss of control over her life, loss of privacy, and imminent illness and death. In reality, remaining in an unsuitable home environment can result in greater loss of independence and privacy, more illness, and a stronger possibility of ending up in a nursing home sooner than if living in a more supportive environment.

How can you alleviate the stress on a parent who needs or wants to make a change in her living arrangement? The first requisite is a great deal of patience. Try to understand her resistance and vacillation, motivated as they are by reluctance to give up what she has and her fears about the unknown situation. And do not expect a reasonable solution to be easily or quickly accepted. Encourage your mom to use the checklists to help her make a decision, and involve her whenever possible in accumulating information on housing alternatives in the area in which she wants to live.

After you have put your heads together and selected the most acceptable choices, both of you should visit each place on the list. Allow enough time for talking with management and residents. If necessary, make several visits so that your mother can familiarize herself with the housing, neighborhood, transportation, shops, and services in the area. If you or your mother have friends or acquaintances who live in some type of communal housing, arrange for her to talk with them.

Try to assure her that the stress and anxiety she may be experiencing are normal, and convince her not to let these feelings stand in the way of making a decision. Explain that the fear and trepidation are only temporary and are certain to pass once she has settled into the new environment.

One good way to ease a prospective move into new housing is to encourage your mom to contact social, religious, or recreational associations or clubs of interest to her and to make any other contacts that will prepare her for living in the new place. This should help her feel more comfortable and settled after she has made the move, and it will keep her busy and perhaps build positive excitement beforehand. Spending some time in the new residence prior to the move, if possible, is the best way for your mother to familiarize herself with the place and its people. It will also give her a good chance to plan the decorating and furnishing of her new quarters.

During the actual preparations for the move, your mom will

need assistance with deciding what to dispose of and what to keep and with sorting and packing. Do this as much in advance and as gradually as possible, so that the job does not seem overwhelming. And after the move, try to be on hand for any initial support she may need in her new home—with socializing, for example, or shopping for new furnishings—and most important, to reassure her that the family is not about to abandon her.

To help a parent who is willing to consider a communal type of living arrangement, several other factors must be taken into account. For example: Your mother values her privacy very highly and would opt for lifetime care, but you both realize she cannot afford the high cost of a life-care community. Well, you still have several alternatives that offer a communal lifestyle with a good deal of privacy and at lower cost: a subsidized housing project (if she qualifies under the income guidelines), congregate housing, or a group-shared home (with, admittedly, a little less privacy).

In addition to individual preferences and financial resources, two other important questions are: Does the kind of housing I'd like exist in the area in which I want to live? Are there long waiting lists?

Finally in deciding which living arrangement is most suitable, you and your mom should consider present and anticipated changes in her ability to handle everyday chores. The following checklist has been adapted from *Your Home, Your Choice: A Workbook for Older People and Their Families*, published by the American Association of Retired Persons (1985).

|  | *Now* | *In 5 Years* | *In 10 Years* |
|---|---|---|---|
| 1. I need help with shopping. | | | |
| 2. I need help with transportation. | | | |
| 3. I need help preparing meals. | | | |
| 4. I need help with light housekeeping. | | | |
| 5. I need help with laundry. | | | |
| 6. I need help with bathing and personal care. | | | |
| 7. I need help in getting around my house. | | | |

|  | | *In 5* | *In 10* |
| --- | --- | --- | --- |
| *(continued)* | *Now* | *Years* | *Years* |

8. I need help with home maintenance.

9. I need help with my finances, such as banking, checkbook, paying bills.

10. I am unable to see friends as often as I would like.

Obviously, the greater the number of yes responses, the greater the need for a supportive environment. Even if future needs are anticipated, as indicated by check marks in the "in 5 years" or "in 10 years" columns, it's not too early to start looking and planning. Because waiting lists are long, it would be wise for your mother to select a suitable housing arrangement and put her name on the waiting list. Waiting too long can imperil her chances for entry. Should she suffer physical losses that impair her ability to live independently or semi-independently and to care for herself, she will no longer meet the entrance requirements for most communal living arrangements. Once again we stress the importance of realism in facing our parents' older years and of helping them plan for the best possible lifestyle while they still can manage.

Assuming that your mother has been sensible and realistic and has decided on a particular housing alternative, your next step is to obtain a list of those available in the geographic areas preferred. (Sources of information and assistance are listed later in this chapter and in the appendices.) You can request brochures from places in the housing category your mother has chosen and, on the basis of these, select the most appealing to visit. Allow enough time on each visit to talk with staff members and residents. Try to stay for at least one main meal and ask to see a weekly menu. Below are some questions your mother will want to ask:

1. Will I be comfortable? Will I feel at home?

2. Are the residents the kind of people with whom I can make friends?

3. Will I be able to maintain my privacy?

4. Will I continue to feel independent and have control over my own life?

5. Do I find the place attractive?

6. Can I bring my own furniture and furnishings?

7. Do I have my own apartment? If not, which rooms do I have to share?

8. Can I pursue my hobbies and recreational activities here? Are there volunteer and work opportunities in the area?

9. Is it near shops, banks, churches, synagogues, and facilities and services? Or does it offer any of these?

10. Does it offer transportation? On what basis and how often? Is it near public transportation?

11. Can I afford the cost? Will I be able to in the future?

12. Does it offer any recreational and cultural programs? Are residents involved in planning and conducting these programs?

13. Is there a residents' association or council? What is its relationship to management?

14. Does it offer meals? How many? Are they mandatory?

15. Is provision made for special dietary needs?

16. Does the residence offer housekeeping and linen services?

17. Does it offer any personal services, such as help with bathing and grooming?

18. Does it offer or will management assist in obtaining home health care, if needed? Does it offer any nursing or medical services?

19. Does it provide for assistance in medical emergencies? Is it located near a hospital?

20. Is it registered or licensed by the state or regulated by any government agency? What is its status?

21. Is it managed by a government agency, a private nonprofit, or a for-profit organization?

22. How long has it been in existence? What is its history? What are the history and reputation of the housing sponsor?

23. What is the financial status of the residence?

24. How do the residents like the housing? Do they seem active and cheerful?

25. Can I live with the rules and regulations?

26. Does the management allow residents enough freedom to pursue their own lifestyles?

27. Will I be able to continue living there for the rest of my life? Or will I have to move if my health deteriorates?

28. Does the residence appear to be clean and well run? Does it provide sufficient security and safety?

29. Are there any restrictions on visitors?

30. What is its reputation with state and local agencies?

It's highly unlikely that all the answers to the above questions will be positive. But they do not need to be completely positive in order for the residence to be acceptable. Different criteria will be more important to certain individuals than to others. In any case, the more information you and your parent can gather, the more comprehensive and realistic the picture both of you will have.

Overall, your parent must first and foremost want to live in the area, be able to afford it (now and in the foreseeable future), find the living conditions attractive, be compatible with the other residents, obtain needed services, and continue to have privacy, independence, and freedom.

What if your mother wishes to move to another area of the state or to another state? Making the move without having spent some time in the area could be a serious mistake. It would be best if she had tried living there for a while, testing her reactions to the climate and familiarizing herself with shopping, transportation, and recreational, cultural, educational, volunteer, and job opportunities. Differences in the cost of living between areas could be important, too. Even if your mother has spent some time in the new part of the country—and especially if she has not—urge her to rent her house or sublet her apartment for at least three to six months while she tries the new arrangement. As a matter of fact, this is a wise precaution to take when making any lifestyle change. Then, if she has great difficulty adjusting, she can go home again.

For the parent who has decided that the best solution is to move in with children, here are some questions to ask:

1. Will I have enough privacy?
2. Will I have my own bedroom? Bath? Sitting/living room to entertain my friends?
3. Can I tolerate the noise, the music, and other activities of grandchildren?
4. Will there be an equitable financial arrangement so that I will be paying a fair share for my living quarters and food?
5. Will I have any say in the menus? Will I do any of the meal preparation?
6. Will I be expected to care for grandchildren? To what extent?
7. Will I be close enough to friends, senior centers, transportation, and recreational and other activities so that I will not be completely dependent on my family for my social life?
8. Will I be able to maintain my "apartness" and not interfere in my children's and grandchildren's lives unless my advice or assistance is requested?

If the answers to the above questions are not satisfactory to you or your parent, then extreme caution is advised in making an arrangement to move your parent into your home.

After all the questioning and soul-searching, there comes a time when your mother has decided whether to stay or to go. And if her decision is to go, she has indicated at least a tentative interest in a particular kind of living arrangement. Now, where do you start the actual search? You start at the source, your state's agency on aging. (State units on aging are listed in appendix I.) The state agency will probably have lists of housing alternatives and programs and may also direct you to the area agency on aging (AAA). Or you can contact the National Association of Area Agencies on Aging in Washington, D.C. for the location of the AAA in the area you are re-searching. (Because there are over 600 area agencies on aging in the United States, it is impractical to list them in this book.)

Most states have an AAA in every region and county except Rhode Island, where the state and area agency are the same unit. Many municipalities also have a department or division on aging that can provide information on current housing alternatives and those in the planning or construction stages. Any one of the units on aging, from town to state, should be able to supply you with lists of differ-ent types of residences and home-sharing programs for older people. In addition, several state units have started consumer education pro-grams to provide information on housing choices for the elderly, as has the American Association for Retired Persons. The AARP effort is called Consumer Housing Information Services for Seniors (CHISS); it will assist communities in setting up programs and will train volunteers to provide information and counseling.

Other good sources of information are state housing finance agencies (listed in appendix III) and county and municipal community-development departments. And if you live in or want to relocate to a rural area, the regional Farmers Home Administration (FmHA) office can help. The number should be listed in the area telephone book; but if you cannot find it, the FmHA, Department of Agricul-ture, Washington, DC 20250, can give you the location of the nearest office.

Other national organizations offering housing information are:

American Association of Retired Persons (AARP)
1909 K Street NW, Washington, DC 20049

National Council on the Aging, Inc. (NCOA)
600 Maryland Avenue SW, West Wing 100,
Washington, DC 20024

American Association of Homes for the Aging (AAHA) and
Continuing Care Accreditation Commission
1129 20 Street NW, Suite 400, Washington, DC 20036
(AAHA-affiliated state associations are listed in appendix II.)

National Council of Senior Citizens (NCSC)
925 15 Street NW, Washington, DC 20005

American Health Care Association
1200 15 Street NW, Washington, DC 20005

National Association of Home Care
205 C Street NE, Washington, DC 20002

National Association of Area Agencies on Aging (N4A)
600 Maryland Avenue SW, Room 208, Washington, DC 20024

National Association of State Units on Aging (NASUA)
600 Maryland Avenue SW, Suite 208, Washington, DC 20024

National organizations that can provide information on specific types of housing alternatives are:

National Center for Home Equity Conversion
110 East Main, Room 1010, Madison, WI 53703
(for information on home-equity conversion)

Shared Housing Resource Center, Inc.
6344 Greene Street, Philadelphia, PA 19144
(for information on home sharing and group-shared homes)

U.S. Department of Housing and Urban Development (HUD)
451 7 Street SW, Washington, DC 20410
(for information on federally subsidized projects for low- and moderate-income elderly)

Additional sources of information and assistance and some selected supplementary readings are given in appendix IV.

While you are conducting your search, it may seem that there is more information available than actual housing. In certain areas of the country, that is true, whereas in others, construction is booming. For example, in Ocean County, New Jersey, already a mecca for retirees by 1986, new development that year included two congregate housing communities—one with 425 apartments and a 60-bed nursing home, the other with 300 apartments and 24-hour nurse and doctor service; a life-care community of 380 units and a 60-bed medical facility; a retirement hotel with 104 rooms; and a retirement village projected to have 2,400 homes.[4]

The area your mother intends to settle in may not be as well endowed with special housing for the elderly. But if, like so many older parents, she wants to live near you and if she is agreeable to sharing a home with an individual or group, you are not as dependent on existing housing programs. There is no reason why you—with your mother if she is willing and able—cannot influence your church, synagogue, or a local service organization, like the Junior League or Lions Club, to initiate a housemate-matching program or a group-shared home project.

Perhaps your parent has old friends who are contemplating changes in their living arrangements. Might they be willing to pool their resources in a group-shared home? All they may need is a nudge from you and some of their younger relatives and some early assistance in finding and renovating a house and hiring housekeeping help. Sound far fetched? It is unusual, to be sure, but look for more and more of these self-help arrangements as long as new-housing costs continue to rise.

In any case, as we said earlier, the choice is not yours to make. You are guiding and supporting your parent in what is essentially her quest. The closer she comes to a safe and happy living arrangement, the better you will both feel. And if, in the process, you learn more about where and how older people live, it is knowledge that should prove very useful now and in the future.

# 8

# Who Are the Elderly?

*A general picture of the older population*

"Something very new is happening in our time . . . the emergence of a large and rapidly growing later-life population," said Dr. Robert N. Butler, noted geriatrician, calling this "the aging revolution, because it raises profound issues and challenges to our society."[1]

Most readers of this book already are well aware of this on a personal level. How can a look at the larger picture help? For one thing, a more comprehensive view can give you a better perspective on your own family's situation. For another, it may clear away some of the myths and false images of aging and the aged that are so prevalent in our youth-oriented society.

The current population of older people in the United States is very different, in both size and character, from elderly populations of the past. It is larger, better educated, more economically secure, and therefore more independent than previous generations. At the same time with more people living longer, increasing numbers of frail and impaired elderly require attention and assistance.

Today's 65-plus population is increasing in relation to the general population, both proportionately and in absolute numbers. The percentage of people age 65 and over relative to the general population has tripled in this century: from 4.1 percent in 1900 to 11.9 percent in 1984. During the same time, their numbers have multiplied by nine: from 3.1 million to 28 million. In 1984, one out of every nine Americans was 65 or older—an increase of 10 percent in just the four years since 1980, while the under-65 population increased by only 4 percent. In fact, the older population has been growing more than twice as fast as the rest of the population for the last two decades, a trend that is expected to continue well into the next century.[2]

Not only is the older population growing, it is also aging. The 75-plus age group (11.3 million in 1984) is currently the fastest-growing segment of the population. This means that it is increasingly likely that an older individual will have a surviving parent and that there will be more and more four- and five-generation families. Already, half of all persons 65 and older have great-grandchildren.

Because life expectancy *at birth* for women is greater than that for men (78.3 years compared with 71 years), elderly women now outnumber elderly men by three to two. This disparity increases with age, so that by age 85 there are ten women for every four men. This is a considerable change in both life expectancy and gender ratio since the early part of the century. A baby born in 1900 could expect to live an *average* of 47.3 years, while a baby born in 1983 could expect to live an *average* of 74.7 years.

Until 1920, the gap in life expectancy between males and females was less than two years. And as early as 1930, there were equal numbers of men and women age 65 and over. In the ensuing years, however, women have outdistanced men in life expectancy.

The upward turn in life expectancy during the first half of this century is attributed to the dramatic reduction in infant and childhood deaths due to infectious diseases; in more recent years, it has been due to decreased mortality among the middle-aged and older population. And anyone who reaches age 65 has a good chance of living beyond the average life expectancy. For example, a woman who celebrated her 65th birthday in 1980 could expect to live another 18 years, and a man could expect to live an additional 14 years.

The marital status of women and men changes significantly as they age. Although more than half of all persons age 65-plus were married and living together in two-person households in 1984, the men were twice as likely to be married as the women (78 percent of men, 40 percent of women). Half of all older women were widows; in fact, there were over five times as many widows as widowers. In the 75-plus age group, only about 20 percent of the women were married, and seven out of ten were widowed, while seven out of ten men were married.

Greater longevity among women and the fact that men tend to marry women younger than themselves create this wide disparity, which appears to be growing. From 1950 to 1980, the ratio of 65-plus married men to widowers changed from two to one to more than four to one. According to the U.S. Census Bureau, "Elderly widowed men have remarriage rates about seven times higher than those of women. The 'average widow' who has not remarried is 65 years old, has been widowed six years, and can expect to live an additional 24 years as a widow."[3]

Perhaps one out of four of these widows will be living near, at, or below the poverty level. Again there is a wide difference between men and women. Median income for older men in 1984 was $10,450; for older women, $6,020. The defined poverty line that year was $6,282 for an older couple and $4,979 for an older individual living alone. About 3.3 million elderly fell below the poverty line (15 percent of the female and 9 percent of the male elderly population), and 2.4 million more were classified as "near poor."[4] In total, over one-fifth (21 percent) of the older population were poor or near poor in 1984. In addition, older persons living alone or with nonrelatives were more likely to be living in poverty (24 percent) than were those living in families (7 percent).

For the elderly population in general, Social Security benefits are the single largest source of cash income. These benefits reach more than 91 percent of the 65-plus population; over 50 percent depend on Social Security for half of their income, and one-fifth receive 90 percent or more of their income from this source.[5]

A sizable proportion of the elderly's income is spent on housing: 19 percent spend at least two-fifths of their income, and another 13 percent spend more than half of their income on housing and utilities. A 1982 Bureau of Labor Statistics (U.S. Department of Labor) report on budgets for retired couples (of all income levels) age 65 and over estimated that housing costs constituted the highest single category of expenses; food was the next highest.[6]

About three-fourths of the elderly owned their own homes in 1980, but this dropped to half for those over 75. And about 80 percent of all elderly homeowners had paid off their mortgages. With advancing age, more older people become renters.

Whether they rent or own, many people 65 and over live in older homes. In 1980, for example, 40 percent of elderly homeowners lived in housing structures built in 1939 or earlier.[7] While the age of the housing need not be an indicator of its condition, it can serve as a measure of its suitability in regard to size, convenience, and ease of maintenance. Indeed, housing studies have shown that many of the elderly live in homes that are too large and too difficult to maintain. In addition, the age of the house affects its market value. The 1981 median value of homes built in 1939 or earlier was $39,000, whereas the median value of homes built after 1970 was $79,000.[8]

Five percent or so of elderly households are in units supplied by the U.S. Department of Housing and Urban Development (HUD) and the Farmers Home Administration (FmHA), a total of 1,377,743 housing units by mid-1982. Although accurate figures countrywide are not available, at least one million are on waiting lists for these federally subsidized units.[9]

Retirement housing—such as congregate and life-care communities, retirement towns and villages, shared-living homes, and retirement hotels—accommodate a variously estimated 5 percent to 15 percent of the elderly (depending on the housing included in this category).

Only about five percent live in institutions, such as nursing homes, at any given time. And it has been estimated that from one-third to one-half of the institutionalized elderly could live in supportive housing in the community if such housing were available. "There is a realization that nursing care and the hospital-like environment of nursing homes are not necessary for many older people who simply need meals prepared, a safe environment, and someone to 'keep an eye on them.' "[10]

In summary, most people (80 to 90 percent) age 65 and over live in ordinary housing (houses, apartments, condominiums) about three-quarters of them in homes they own, many of which were built 50 or more years ago. As older individuals and their homes age, however, problems that are increasingly difficult to cope with tend to arise. At the same time, income tends to fall and health needs to rise, creating additional hardships that contribute to a general decline in the ability to function independently.

Although the majority of older people today perceive of themselves as being in good health, most have at least one chronic condition, and many have multiple conditions. Of the 65-plus population who are not in institutions, 50 percent have arthritis, about 40 percent have hypertension, 26 percent have heart conditions, and 9 percent are diabetic. Hearing, orthopedic, and visual impairments also afflict many of the elderly. This contrasts with the earlier years of this century, when acute ailments predominated and few people lived long enough to develop chronic conditions.

The major causes of death among the elderly in the United States in 1984 were heart disease, cancer, and stroke, which together account for the deaths of three out of four persons age 65 and over. Heart disease, in fact, is the number-one cause of death in all age groups, including the elderly. Over the last decade, however, deaths due to heart disease and stroke have decreased, while those due to cancer have increased.

According to recent national health surveys, about 18 percent of the elderly report they are no longer able to care for their own basic needs. Of course, the percentage of disabled increases with age. Fourteen percent of the 65-to-74 age group and 23 percent of the 75-plus group (outside of those in nursing homes) need help with shopping, chores, meals, and managing money.[11]

Families always have been and continue to be the main providers of service and care for impaired and disabled elderly—a spouse, if there is one, or another member of the family, most often a daughter or daughter-in-law. Community services are an important supplement to family efforts and a vital necessity for those elderly who have no family to rely on. "Lack of community services can place more stress on the family than it can bear," said one gerontologist, adding, "indeed, one recent study . . . shows that the coordination of formal and informal support networks *enhances* the quality of family care."[12]

Yet of the 10 percent of 65-plus households having one or more persons at risk of institutionalization, two-thirds receive no housing-related support services, such as personal care, meals, homemaking, chore assistance, home maintenance, transportation, housing search assistance or other information and referral services.[13]

Income falls among the elderly, in part because of retirement from jobs and in part because of increased spending for health care. Only about 11 percent of the elderly were in the work force (working or actively seeking work) in the mid-1980s; approximately half were part-time workers, and one-quarter were self-employed.

Personal health-care expenditures for the elderly were about $120 billion in 1984—31 percent of the national total. On average, $4,202 was spent for each person 65 and older, more than three times the $1,300 spent for each younger person. Hospital expenses accounted for the largest share (45 percent). More than twice as many older persons were hospitalized during the year than were persons under 65 (20 percent compared with 9 percent); the elderly were also more likely to have more than one hospital stay per year and to have longer stays. As may be expected, the 65-plus age group averaged more physician visits: eight to five compared with the rest of the population.

Medicare paid almost half the 1984 national health-care bill for the elderly. Medicare is government insurance that provides payment for medical and hospital care from federal Social Security funds. Anyone over 65 is eligible for Medicare, regardless of income. The program has two parts: Part A automatically pays most hospital-care costs; Part B is medical insurance paid for by a monthly premium deducted from Social Security payments and is optional.

Medicaid, which is financed jointly by the federal government and the states, is an assistance program for eligible low-income people of all ages. It is a much more comprehensive program than Medicare, covering all kinds of medical and hospital costs. Medicaid paid approximately one-eighth of the elderly's health care costs in 1984, and other government sources (e.g., Veterans Administration, Department of Defense, states, and counties) paid another eighth. The elderly themselves paid one-quarter of the total. Their out-of-pocket expenses were actually the same in 1984 as they were prior to the enactment in 1965 of Medicare and Medicaid, averaging just over $1,000 annually for each older person (not including payments for Medicare B and private insurance premiums). But the number of physician visits and the percentage of the elderly who saw physicians during one year rose significantly since Medicare started, particularly among lower-income groups.

More than two-thirds of the Medicaid dollar spent on the elderly went to nursing homes, but half of all nursing-home expenses were paid by patients and their families. Eligibility requirements for Medicaid are set by each state. To qualify, individuals must exhaust their own financial resources. Many states, however, protect family income and assets that do not belong to the patient herself. A widespread, erroneous belief is that Medicare will pay all or part of the bill for a nursing-home patient. In fact, Medicare pays for only 100 days of care, not for long-term custodial care.

Again, we emphasize that only a small percentage of the elderly (5 percent) are in nursing homes and that, despite the prevalence of chronic conditions, most elderly persons live in the community and manage to remain more or less independent into their 80s and 90s. It may be a struggle, especially for the women, but they do it. We focus on the women because there are more of them, they have substantially lower incomes and higher poverty rates, and they are much more likely to be widowed and living alone. Only a small number can be classified as well-to-do, with annual incomes in excess of $35,000 (1 percent as compared with 5 percent of elderly men).

The older woman has usually suffered a series of losses on the way to living alone—loss of spouse and friends, loss of her role as homemaker and as jobholder. Widowhood brings with it grief, loneliness, depression, and the need to cope alone with problems formerly shared. Many older women are also called upon to be caregivers for ailing husbands and parents while at the same time confronted by their own health and career problems and by family problems relating to children and grandchildren.

Demographic reality, therefore, gives us this bare-bones portrait of the aging woman: "Outliving her husband, maintaining an independent residence, remaining in contact with offspring and kin, and surviving through the eighth decade. As she grows old, the possibility of increased frailty, depletion of personal and financial resources, and the scarcity of suitable, safe accommodations will render problematic her continued ability to function independently."[14]

Such information should demolish the myth of a world full of rich old widows. What are some of the other myths about aging? One persistent idea is that age inevitably brings mental deterioration. Yet recent studies have shown that the elderly scored just as high as younger persons in verbal intelligence tests, and the researchers concluded that language and verbal abilities hold up very well into old age. Reaction time may be slower, they said, but once the material is learned, it is retained well. Creative abilities also continue into old age, not only for major talents like Pablo Picasso, George Bernard Shaw, and Artur Rubinstein, but for the average person as well.[15]

Some memory loss does occur with aging, but senility or cognitive impairment is not an attribute of normal aging; it is a result of disease, such as Alzheimer's disease, the leading cause of cognitive impairment in the elderly. National Institutes of Mental Health (NIMH) studies found mild cognitive impairment in about 14 percent of noninstitutionalized elderly and severe impairment in 5.6 percent of elderly men and 3 percent of elderly women. On the other hand, NIMH also has found that the elderly had the lowest rates of all other age groups for most other mental disorders, such as schizophrenia, phobias, and substance abuse. Poor nutrition, depression, and adverse reactions to medications can cause symptoms of senility, but the condition is usually reversible when the underlying causes have been corrected.[16]

Badly deteriorated physical functioning as a necessary element of old age is also a false image. Even after age 80, only about 20 percent of the population lives in nursing homes. Despite their chronic conditions, which vary greatly in effect among individuals, most elderly over 80 live in their own homes and manage their daily affairs and activities. Just how many of those in nursing homes could have continued to live in their communities if suitable supportive housing were available is an open question.

As for the old saw that women are happiest when they are fulfilling their primary roles as homemakers, child guardians, and spouse helpmates: that, too, is being called into question. Though some women thrive in these roles, others find they need the additional self-esteem that comes with an outside job. In many cases, of course, the motivating force is economic need. "For employed women, the centrality of work to their lives . . . was found to have a powerful positive impact upon psychological well-being." For many women, the benefits of multiple roles last into later life, even when they are alone.[17]

Modern women of all ages have made this discovery and—whether for reasons of self-fulfillment or economic need—more of them are now in the work force than ever before. This has reinforced the myth that older people are losing contact with their children, who are said to be too busy with their own lives and careers to make time for parents. Not so, the data tell us. Four-fifths of the elderly have one or more surviving children. When a survey was conducted by the Administration on Aging, 75 percent of elderly persons said they had seen at least one child within the week, and only 11 percent had not seen a child in the previous month. Of the people living alone, 23 percent saw a child daily; an additional 40 percent saw a child at least once a week, half of them more than once a week. Only 3 percent said they never saw a child or saw one less than once a year.

In any case, a large majority of all elderly people have frequent telephone contacts with their children. Among the substantial portion of elderly who live alone and have no living children (29 percent in 1984) or only one child (19 percent), the potential for isolation is much greater.

Close relationships between children and older parents, however, do not ensure provision of care for several reasons. First, the neediest and fastest-growing age group is the very old—85 and over. The children of these aged parents are elderly themselves and may not have the physical or financial resources to provide needed care. Additionally, smaller family size has meant fewer children to share the burden. Lastly, many more of the traditional caregivers, the women, are in the work force rather than at home and cannot be counted on for full-time assistance to elderly parents.

Nevertheless, employed women appear to give their elderly widowed mothers as much affective support as do daughters who are not employed, according to a study done a few years ago in Philadelphia. Somehow, working daughters found the time to help with all the usual chores except personal care and meals, for which they hired other providers. As wage earners, they were able to pay aides for this care. The same researcher found, in a later study, that "28 percent of the nonworking daughters interviewed had quit their jobs to take care of their disabled mothers, and some of the women who were still working had reduced their working hours or were thinking of quitting."[18]

Despite the bond between children and parents and their willingness to help each other, providing help on a continuous basis places a strain on these relationships. Changes associated with aging are difficult to understand and to accept for the older person and for the family. The passage from autonomy to greater dependency, for example, creates feelings of guilt in the parent for "being a burden" and in the child for "not being able to do enough."

Changes in the personal and social life of an older individual can alter her self-image—from wife to widow, worker to dependent, active to sedentary, socializer to isolate—and with that her personality. As more positive life roles slip away, family and friends take on added significance. She may eventually come to define herself strictly in terms of her place in the family unless she has a few good friends among her peers.

Peer friendships are especially important to an older person. Having lived through the same historical era, friends share similar memories and life experiences. And having experienced hard times themselves, friends can offer the kind of support and sympathy in times of illness and trouble that younger family members are not equipped by their life experiences to do. Friends can also strengthen immunity against social prejudice and intolerance; they are slow together, and they can laugh or cry about their forgetfulness or aches and pains as they would not with others. Role models for successful aging can be found among friends as well, and new self-images can be developed. Family tensions may also be relieved if emotional and social dependency is divided with friends.

Most valuable of all, many older people say, is an intimate friend, someone to whom they can confide their innermost feelings, their hopes and fears. For many widows, the loss of a husband is most keenly felt as the loss of that "significant other." No matter how full life is of activity and people, they miss the closeness and tolerance of a partner who accepts them, foibles and all, and who listens and responds with empathy, understanding, and affection.

A close relationship with a child is not an adequate substitute, though it can be a lovely friendship on its own terms. And with more children of elderly parents entering their senior years, many more of these children will have common experiences and greater understanding of mutual problems.

A woman who has based much of her identity on her marital relationship is most vulnerable to loneliness after the death of her husband. Years of defining herself almost exclusively as a wife will have created a self-image that is shattered by widowhood. Divorce, which is increasing even in the 65-plus population, can be even more devastating because it is a blow to the ego as well. The emotional support of family and friends is desperately needed to help the widow or divorcee recover her equilibrium and build a new self-image.

Other women (and men), by contrast, surprise friends and family by behaving as if they had been released from bondage after the death of a spouse. They blossom as more independent and self-reliant than ever before, no longer willing to be subordinate to anyone. Even these older people, however, will need a support structure and an appropriate living arrangement, possibly a new one to go with the newfound personality.

Throughout the life cycle, school, work, family, friends, and formal and informal organizations provide us with opportunities for social interaction, social activity, and community involvement. In our present society, however, extreme social-role changes are brought on by retirement, by loss of spouse and other close family members and friends, and by decreased functional ability. Usually, the more advanced the age, the more extreme the changes. One result is the social isolation of many elderly, an involuntary isolation that often leads to loneliness.

Some changes in the aging person are genetically or physically determined: diminution of vision, hearing, and muscle strength, and disease. Other changes, such as marital status and loss of spouse, family, and friends, are determined by circumstance. Still other changes, such as retirement, may be imposed by society. The elderly who are more prone to social isolation tend to be of lower socioeconomic status, in poorer health, retired, single or widowed, older, and without children or other relatives living nearby. Usually, it is a combination of these factors, rather than any one factor, that produces isolation.

Many of society's attitudes and policies, if changed, could reduce social isolation for the elderly. But the provision of meaningful substitute roles and improved self-image would go a long way toward ending the isolation and the resulting loneliness. That is why living arrangements are so important, especially for the older elderly who are living alone. The type of housing, its location, and opportunities for social interaction and friendship can play a crucial role in reducing isolation and loneliness, in increasing psychological well-being, and in maintaining independence.

A communal type of living arrangement offers much in the way of support services that can help an older person remain independent and assume new social roles and improve her self-image. Extensive research on subsidized housing projects, congregate housing, and life-care communities indicates that residents live longer, healthier, happier lives than their counterparts living alone in their own houses and apartments. For example, one study of a subsidized housing project in San Francisco showed how substitute work roles developed as a result of volunteer activities, such as fundraising for a local women's club, visits to nearby nursing homes, and constructing yarn dolls for an orphanage. These activities and others stimulated by the housing environment served an important function in structuring the residents' social relations.[19]

In an earlier book describing research done at a life-care community, we (the authors) arrived at similar conclusions. Through its residents' council and its location in a downtown area, the community provided many of its residents with meaningful substitute roles as volunteers, workers, leaders, committee members, friends. Increased social interaction and new friendships were stimulated by communal dining, informal cocktail hours, and a diversity of recreational and hobby activities.[20]

Despite the known advantages of specially designed housing, shared housing, and group living arrangements for the elderly, most older people still want to continue living where they are. This is no less true for many who are frail and have physical disabilities, or who pay 35 percent or more of their income for housing, or who live alone in deteriorating neighborhoods. Resistance to moving is one of the major obstacles to seeking better housing alternatives. Another prime problem is that housing choices may be severely limited by long waiting lists or may not even exist in the area where they are wanted.

Resistance to moving stems, in part, from the cultural norm in our society that dictates that remaining in one's own home confers higher status and better self-image than making a move to an "old folks' home." Many housing alternatives for the elderly are, therefore, viewed negatively by them and, too often, by their families as well. Adult children imbued with this common prejudice and who suffer feelings of guilt when faced with the possibility of parents' moving into group living arrangements add to this resistance. As these housing arrangements become more familiar and understanding of their advantages increases, this attitude is slowly changing.

A 1980 housing survey of 1,300 older households found that about one out of ten older households moved from one private residence to another within the previous two years. Another two out of ten households wished to move during that time but did not. Personal or family reasons for moving were given most frequently. Other major reasons were housing quality, neighborhood, and other locational factors.

Among the nonmovers who wished to move, the majority gave reasons for not moving that related to the economics of housing: the cost of housing, the costs of moving or buying and selling real estate, or the availability of alternative housing. Many expressed interest in "nontraditional" housing alternatives. One-third of the homeowners and one-third of the renters were interested in housing that offered personal-care services; 6 to 8 percent were interested in each of the following options: reverse-annuity financing, partial conversion of the home into rental units, house sharing, and living in a boarding home. Among renters, 10 percent expressed interest in house sharing, and 6 percent in living in "a rooming house."[21]

A study of people over the age of 70 living in various sections of the country found that twice as many had made housing changes before age 70 than afterward. It was also learned that the longer a widow stayed in place after her husband's death, the less likely she was to move. And if the spouse died suddenly, a move was more likely than if a terminal illness was prolonged.[22]

Why do the overwhelming majority of elderly people prefer to stay in their own homes? Societal perceptions (as we noted earlier), personal beliefs and perceptions, and housing realities are all part of the answer.

Many older persons expect their existing informal support systems (family and friends) to continue, no matter how their needs change. Though not always realistic, this perception would tend to discourage any move. Also, many think that housing alternatives for the elderly are good expedients for others but not for them. A third perception is that their present housing is better than any alternative could be.

In most cases, these perceptions are rationalizations for a strong attachment to the home in which the person has lived for many years. Home is a known quantity, familiar and loved, associated with life history and fond memories. After long residence, the individual has probably adapted to any shortcomings and feels comfortable with the familiar neighborhood, friends, shops, and services. A parent's home may also be seen as the focal point of family life, the place where children and other family members can gather. By contrast, most housing alternatives are unknown and unfamiliar and, therefore, frightening.

Any move or change in living arrangement engenders physical and emotional stress. And as a person ages and has less energy to cope with change, the stress increases. Most elderly do not want or are unable to face the challenge of looking for housing alternatives, making the change, and adjusting to the new situation. Since most moves are made into smaller quarters, there is the added stress of making decisions about what belongings to dispose of and what to take to the new home. And after that comes the necessary adjustment to living in a smaller space.

Before an individual ever reaches the stage of choosing and moving, she may well be confronted by a scarcity of options in the area. The major reason for the inadequate supply is the steep rise in the 65-plus population (and even more in the 75-plus segment), resulting in unprecedented demand, especially for units in low- and moderate-income subsidized housing projects. At the same time, all social programs, including low and moderate income housing, have been severely curtailed. With the exception of housing vouchers (to be used by the poor to pay for existing housing), no government subsidies are anticipated for new construction or for rehabilitation of old housing units. Without these subsidies or other government incentives, it will be difficult to attract private builders or private capital to develop housing alternatives, particularly for the not-so-affluent elderly.

Another serious obstacle comes in the form of zoning laws. In many localities, zoning laws are so restrictive they effectively prohibit accessory apartments, elder cottages, group-shared homes, and other housing alternatives. Lengthy and costly zoning variance applications and procedures are required and, in the end, permission is often denied.

The growing older population is a fact of life our society must learn to live with. In regard to funding and zoning restrictions, however, the public can (and should) take action. Pressure can be applied on all levels of government to provide funds and other incentives that will encourage private and nonprofit developers to build and renovate housing wherever it is in short supply. For middle- and upper-income groups, and to a lesser extent those of moderate income, the private and nonprofit sector is picking up some of the slack, as demonstrated by the growing number of home-sharing programs, group-shared living arrangements, and congregate and life-care communities.

Zoning laws are also subject to change by public pressure. This "uniquely American approach to protection of property values has become a widely accepted practice with valid objectives. But greater flexibility—and uniformity—may be needed."[23]

The most onerous zoning restrictions, in the opinion of housing alternative advocates, are those that regulate the composition of households. Regulating land use is felt to be a legitimate concern of municipalities, but restricting living arrangements within households to a narrow and traditional definition of family is condemned as an invasion of basic rights. In some states, courts have ruled against these restrictions, but they have been upheld in others.

Whatever the zoning laws happen to be, remember that they are not immutable. If they are too restrictive, action can be initiated within fraternal, religious, or other community organizations interested in the problem. If enough people share the same point of view, pressure can be applied to the local government to amend the zoning ordinance or to grant a special use permit.

# 9

# Journey's End

THIS book began with the story of a mother and daughter embarking on a search for a new living arrangement for the older woman, a widow, who was unhappy living alone.

Edna, 78 years old and largely self-educated, had been active all her adult life in community, educational, and political affairs. An enthusiastic sailor and crack tennis player as well, she had many friends and respectful competitors—including her daughter, Carol.

Mother and daughter were very close. Both had lived in the same New York shore town throughout their lives, their roots deep in the community. Edna had encouraged Carol to choose a career, to finish college, and to return to work while her two sons were still in grade school. Although Carol never achieved the full training she needed to be an architect, she received her bachelor's degree and qualified as an architectural designer. In community affairs, she followed her mother's lead at first and soon became a worthy ally and an activist in her own right.

Snapping back after the sudden death of her husband 20 years before, Edna had sold her house, moved to a garden apartment, and accelerated the already hectic pace of her life with more meetings, travel, and other activities. As she approached her mid-70s, however, hypertension and cataracts began to slow her down. Then, after several unsuccessful eye operations left her with sharply reduced vision, she was forced to give up driving. Dependent on others for transportation, she gradually withdrew from most of her former activities, including sailing and tennis, the sports she loved most.

Despondent over her relative isolation and inactivity, Edna began neglecting her personal appearance and her apartment. Carol

tried to help, but Edna continued to retreat into self-centered brooding and depression. Upset by the changes in her mother, Carol chal-
lenged her to revive some of the old fighting spirit for an investigation of possible alternatives to living alone. When we left them at the
end of chapter 1, they were in the process of gathering information
from local and regional agencies on aging and on housing.

Initially, Edna had believed few options were open to her: to
move in with Carol and her husband, to move to a retirement community, or to move into a nursing home. She had firmly rejected
living in her daughter's home, remembering the many years her own
mother had lived in her home. She felt that both she and Carol's
family needed space between them and the freedom to follow their
differing lifestyles. (Her son-in-law had expressed similar sentiments
to his wife.) As for the others, retirement-community living required
more strength and energy than she had, and she was still not helpless
enough for a nursing home.

Among the first new alternatives Edna and Carol discussed was
home sharing. A good county-sponsored agency, run by a regional
community-services organization, could help Edna find a home
sharer or a home to share. But Edna had so many objections that
both possibilities were soon abandoned.

"Anyone who came to live in this apartment with me would have
to take care of all the housekeeping. But I doubt that a good housekeeper would be a good companion for me. We'd drive each other
crazy," Edna reasoned. "On the other hand, if she were someone I
could relate to intellectually, she'd probably be a lousy housekeeper,
and there'd be two of us messing up the place instead of one."

Carol thought Edna also dreaded the thought of fixing up the
apartment so it would be more habitable. The spare bedroom was
crammed with books, files, furniture, and all the overflow from the
other three rooms and would have to be cleared out and redecorated.

As far as sharing another person's home, Edna's reservations
about compatibility versus housekeeping were equally valid, unless
she could find some cultured, wealthy person with a household staff.
"But I imagine such people are in rather short supply, at least anyone
who would be willing to share her home with an old lady like me,"
Edna quipped. "Besides, I have a friend who had a bad experience
sharing another woman's home. The owner made a virtual slave of
her. She didn't have enough energy to move out by herself, but finally she got her children to take her out of there."

Subsidized housing projects especially designed for the elderly were next on the list of options. Within the 50-mile radius they had set for themselves, there were only two garden-apartment complexes that met their criteria—not too large and not in congested urban centers. Further investigation revealed that one was a low-income project for which Edna would not qualify. The other, built for moderate-income elderly, was about 45 miles away. A telephone call to the project manager established that there were more than 300 people on the waiting list for 92 occupied apartments. Anyone applying that day would have at least a seven-year wait, much too long for a woman of 78 who was anxious to make a change.

In any case, Carol had doubts about the suitability of this living arrangement: "A new apartment might be an improvement, but it wouldn't solve any of my mother's basic problems with housekeeping and cooking. I felt she needed more support than a project could provide."

Carol thought a life-care community would be better but was surprised to learn that this housing-plus-continuing-care arrangement was prohibited by law in New York State. "I was told that the law against long-term contractual agreements for nursing care was passed about 25 years ago. It was done to protect people against misrepresentations and financial risks," Carol explained.

As residents of a tristate area, however, the two women were able to consider life-care communities in the neighboring states of New Jersey and Connecticut. In addition, there were congregate residences in all three states. In New York, some of these had been built by service organizations that also ran health-related and nursing-care facilities where congregate housing residents could reasonably expect a place if the need arose.

Narrowing the list to three life-care communities and four congregate residences in convenient locations, Edna sent for descriptive literature and price lists. Upon receipt of the information, Edna and Carol eliminated the life-care communities and two of the congregate residences as too expensive. The two remaining congregate residences were costly, but the women calculated that Edna could just manage the monthly fee on her Social Security payments supplemented by the interest on bonds and savings. Both congregate residences had waiting lists: the closer one for three to four years, the other for two to three years. They chose the closer place for their first visit.

Although the Connecticut town was within their mileage limit, heavy traffic made the drive discouragingly slow. Edna and Carol found the high-rise building in a former industrial section that was undergoing renewal and was full of the dust and noise of construction. The 21-story building, towering above the gouged-out landscape, had 254 apartments (studio and one- and two-bedroom). From the roof gardens, an attractive, glass-enclosed sitting area, they could see several towns and the surrounding countryside; to the south, they saw the harbor, Long Island Sound, and even the opposite shore, where they tried to discern their own home town.

Residents seemed lively and busy: going places in vans and cars, engaging in hobby activities in workrooms on the main floor, reading in a pleasant small library, or playing cards. After touring the building with the manager, mother and daughter joined the residents for lunch in the huge second-floor dining room filled with the murmur of polite conversation. Although they had seen some apartments earlier, they gladly accepted an invitation from a woman at their table to visit her apartment after lunch.

Mrs. G—— looked younger than Edna, but said she was 83. She proudly showed them through the two rooms, pointing out furniture and bric-a-brac and relating their histories—a bookcase made by her husband, who had died eight years before, an ornate clock from a trip to Switzerland, a lamp made by her grandson, pillows in cases embroidered by her daughter, and framed watercolors she had painted since moving into the residence the year before. After a half-hour of this, Carol, seeing the impatient look on Edna's face, made their excuses, thanked Mrs. G——, and left with her mother.

"What a ninny!" Edna exclaimed as soon as the apartment door had closed behind them.

"Oh, Mother. You're so intolerant. She was only trying to be friendly," Carol half scolded.

In the stop-and-go traffic of the drive home, Edna delivered her opinions. The location was fine, and when the construction was completed, she thought it might even be "quaint and pretty." She especially liked the view of the harbor and of the boats and ships on the sound. The apartments were small—she understood that was necessary—but were nice enough. "The same goes for the people. Because I'm sure I could find a few who are interested in something other than their possessions," Edna declared. "But just think of it—

almost 300 old people concentrated in one building. It's overwhelming! I'd have to go out and find some young people to talk to. And even then, I'm not sure I could stand living with so many people at once, young or old."

She also admitted that the idea of living in a high-rise building frightened her, although she felt she could probably get used to it. The financial factor worried her, too, she insisted, because she felt her income was barely up to the pay-out required.

For Carol, the major drawback was the congested traffic pattern. But she empathized with her mother's uneasiness over high-rise living and an environment populated by hundreds of old people. The advantages were many, however, and it was these she emphasized.

"You're right about the location, Mother. When the shops and offices and townhouses are finished, it should be great. And I think the residence building itself is clean, attractive, and well laid out. You'd have two meals a day in the dining room, your apartment cleaned and linens changed once a week, and plenty of time for bridge and discussion groups and whatever else grabs you. There are so many ongoing activities, and you heard the manager say that residents are always initiating new ones." Carol continued listing the benefits: transportation to shopping malls, museums, concerts, and theaters; emergency buzzers and check calls; possibilities for new friendships and community involvement.

The second congregate-housing community they looked at was farther from home, in a suburban town to the north. Two- and three-story buildings made it more like the garden-apartment complex in which Edna lived, except that the exteriors were wood instead of brick. The grounds were park-like, and gardens behind the buildings were tended by residents who enjoyed gardening.

Although Edna and Carol liked the layout, they noticed that the buildings, about ten years old, were shabby and poorly maintained; the apartments seemed to be in similar condition. This led them to suspect financial difficulties. The residents also seemed older and less animated than those at the first congregate community.

Before they left, Carol asked for the latest financial statement. The manager claimed he had no copies on hand, but promised to call the corporate treasurer and have it sent to her. She received the statement almost two months later, whereupon she showed it to her lawyer, who confirmed her suspicions.

Meanwhile, as a result of both visits and their previous explorations of possible options, Edna—with Carol's encouragement—decided to sign up for the high-rise congregate residence. A $100 deposit was required to put her name on the waiting list for a studio apartment; it was fully refundable if she withdrew before an apartment became available. When an apartment was free, she would have to submit a complete application with a medical report and a financial statement. If she was then accepted and she refused the apartment, half the deposit would be returned.

Both women felt this was a sensible step, but neither was happy about the long waiting period. Edna was especially impatient and grew more and more irritable over living alone. One day she expressed this irritation to a young woman, a graduate student in sociology, who was helping to run a seminar on aging at her church. "What really ticks me off," Edna said, "is the scarcity of good alternatives for people like me. I don't want to leave this town, but I may be forced to because I can't stand living alone and I don't want to live with my kids."

Betty agreed that housing was a serious problem for many older people, but she thought the solution might lie in the community itself. "I just came back from a visit to my granny in Florida. She recently moved into a house with nine other older people. It's a big remodeled house in an older section of town. Each person has a bedroom, shares a bath with one or two others, and they all use the same living room, dining room, and kitchen. There's a housekeeper, who shops and cooks most of the meals and lives in the house, so if there's any trouble she's there to help. The people eat meals together and try to act like a family, helping each other and the housekeeper. A cleaning service does the heavy housework, but the residents keep their own rooms in order."

Edna thought it "a most interesting idea" and discussed it with Carol the next time she saw her. "Do you know of any shared homes like that around here?" she wondered.

Carol laughed and said, "Not in this town. The zoning's too tight. I know the zoning board recently refused to grant a variance to the mental-health agency when they tried to set up a small group home for retarded adults. But let's talk to the reverend and see if he has any ideas."

After church service on Sunday morning, Betty joined them to talk to the minister. He was impressed with the idea of a group of elderly people sharing a house and said it was certainly worth investigating. He suggested that the four of them form the nucleus of a committee to bring the matter to the attention of the congregation and invite others to join them. So began the Committee on Housing for the Elderly.

An announcement in the monthly newsletter aroused considerable interest. To prepare for the first committee meeting, the nucleus group made an informal survey of regional referral agencies—social service, family counseling, registered nursing, hospitals, and nursing homes. As expected, there was universal agreement from the professionals on the need for noninstitutional supportive housing for the community's elderly. Several social workers offered to join the committee and were welcomed.

The committee then set about gathering information on other community efforts and invited speakers to describe their experiences and the results of their endeavors. Interest grew, and more people, church members and others, joined the housing committee. Five months after its formation, the committee resolved to tackle a small group-shared home project. An attorney drafted incorporation papers and a set of bylaws that were subsequently approved and adopted. The nonprofit corporation, called BLES (Better Living for the Elderly through Sharing), stated as its main purpose: "To provide elderly persons, on a cooperative family basis, with housing facilities and services especially designed to meet their physical, social, and psychological needs, and through the 'caring' second-family environment, to promote their health, security, happiness, and usefulness in longer living."

Officers and a board of directors were elected, and people signed up to work on subcommittees on finance, real estate, public relations, and residents. Carol worked with the real-estate group, Edna with the public-relations and residents' committees. Meanwhile, Edna made an important decision: she moved from her apartment into a rooming house.

"I realized it was going to take at least two years before BLES found and finished a house. And I was fed up with my apartment—hated it every time I walked through the door. Also, I figured I might as well get rid of most of my junk—had to, sooner or later—and see what it was like to live in one room," Edna explained.

The rooming house, in an adjacent town and not far from a state university campus, was owned by a middle-aged divorcee who worked in the campus administration offices. Betty, another woman graduate student, and a young male bank teller were the other three lodgers. "It's still pretty lonely during the day," Edna lamented. "But at least there's someone around most evenings and at night."

Carol worried at first about her mother's meals, since the nutrition center Edna had been attending was now too far away. But the landlady kept the refrigerator well stocked and cooked excellent dinners for herself, Edna, and any of the others who might be around. "Best of all," Carol said, "Mother found out about a bus to the campus that stops right around the corner. On nice days, she goes to the library and reads or listens to tapes. Sometimes Betty meets her and takes her to the cafeteria for lunch. Otherwise, I think she skips lunch. That crowd of students is just too much for her to face alone. All in all, I think she's doing pretty well, certainly less depressed than she was before."

By the time Edna moved, BLES's real-estate committee had looked at more than a dozen houses and made bids on three of them. Carol recalled: "The first was a grand old Victorian on the other side of town. But the owner got cold feet when the neighbors mounted a well-organized and vigorous protest. They rejected the idea of a group home out-of-hand. No matter that its prospective tenants might be their own mothers and fathers. They threatened to take us to court, so we dropped it. We had better things to do with our money, which was going to be very hard to come by anyway."

Forewarned about neighborhood resistance by other sponsors who had encountered it, the housing committee did not allow itself to be discouraged. Instead, it used the opportunity to educate the townspeople. The public relations committee prepared a brochure describing shared, small group homes for the elderly and countering opposition arguments that they lowered property values, placed a strain on community resources, and did not pay their way in taxes. Edna, working with the group, rejoiced at being back in "the battle."

A second house bid was lost when the seller received a higher bid. Finally, a third bid was accepted by a friendly owner with co-operative neighbors who raised no objections. Before the sale could be completed, however, funds had to be found and a zoning variance approved. Housing-committee volunteers went into high gear.

Financing came from several sources. A foundation affiliated with the central office of the church provided start-up funds, a commercial bank provided the first mortgage, and 19 individuals pooled funds for a second mortgage.

The legal committee handled the closing on the purchase of the house and the stickier question of the zoning variance. Application for the variance raised the basic question about whether shared living by persons unrelated by blood or marriage violated single-family residence restrictions. Legal precedents were uncertain, and the town could have contested the variance on that basis. But the matter was resolved in favor of the project, and the variance was granted without undue delay.

"At that point," Carol continued, "the real-estate committee became the building committee and began working with the board and an architect to plan renovations to the house. That was the easy part. Much more time consuming and frustrating was the process of applying for and getting all the necessary building permits, licenses, and authorizations. All that red tape, all those agency hearings and bureaucratic confrontations—that's what really slowed things down."

Additional funds needed for remodeling and renovations and to cover carrying costs were obtained through a community-development grant. Mail and direct-contact appeals for personal and corporate contributions also generated funds to be used for furnishings and interim financing. A mandated sprinkler system was paid for by funding from the state housing finance authority. Another church and several town organizations provided funds for unanticipated needs as the project moved along.

And move along it did. BLES served as its own general contractor; that is, the building committee was empowered to obtain bids, enter into contracts, and perform follow-up. As Carol described the remodeling phase: "It required constant attention, diplomacy, threats, entreaties, even flattery on occasion. We had to watch the construction with an eye to safety, energy conservation, appearance, quality, and cost. It took much longer than we expected."

Volunteers did all the interior painting and decorating. Cooperative professional painters provided instruction and guidance and did the jobs requiring the greatest skill. Unofficial estimates valued this "sweat equity" at $14,000. And the volunteers reported the cooperative experience as fun and personally rewarding.

Two years and five months after the church housing committee held its first meeting, an open house was held, and Edna and another woman became the first two residents to move into Willow Walk. It would be seven months more before the house was fully occupied.

Throughout the months of remodeling, an extensive promotional effort was made to spread the news. Notices were sent to area newspapers, hospitals, social-service agencies, senior centers, churches, synagogues, libraries, businesses and other community organizations; circulars were printed; and a speakers' bureau was set up. Despite the widespread coverage, the response from older people who might need the housing was slow.

"The idea was too new to be readily acceptable," Edna explained. "All the literature we put out and all our speakers emphasized that Willow Walk *would not* be a nursing home or institution of any kind, that it *would* be a home shared by eight older people living together with a live-in homemaker. We played up the family-style atmosphere of a private home. And we tried to capitalize on the fact that living together is not just for the young, since we knew there was general awareness of sharing arrangements among college kids and young people just starting out."

The finished brochure describing Willow Walk offers "independence, dignity, and privacy when you want it, and friendship and mutual support when you want that." It promises furnished public rooms for eating, sitting, and recreation; eight bedrooms that can be furnished by individual residents to their own liking; and a live-in staff to take care of cooking, cleaning, housekeeping, chores, and maintenance. Residents are to be selected for their compatibility by a residents' committee and will be people who are 62 years of age or older, ambulatory, and able to attend to their personal needs. The monthly charge to cover living quarters, food, housekeeping, utilities, and other household expenses is intended to be moderate, the brochure states, but may have to be adjusted from time to time as costs change.

An internal policy statement adopted by the BLES corporate board clarifies its position relative to a resident who lives in the house and is later unable to pay the monthly charge. In such a case, it says, the corporation will pay the cost from its own reserves, from government funds, from funds solicited from other sources, or from a combination of these.

The policy statement contains an excellent expression of the corporation's purpose: "To provide facilities and services to meet the needs of the elderly (1) for affordable family-type living that provides housing, meals, and other household services, (2) oversight of residents' well-being and help in obtaining health care, and (3) optimum protection against the financial risks associated with later years of life. . . . To this end, it is BLES's policy to maintain an attractive residence . . . a family-type atmosphere for congenial supportive relationships and thus help overcome the loneliness of old age."

The residents' committee, which drew up the policy statement, also developed the necessary forms—an invitation to apply, application blank, emergency form, authorization to obtain medical information, physician's report, house rules (including resident's signed acceptance), and occupancy agreement.

The house rules are simple, relating to the use of the house telephone, smoking, laundry, keys, meals, and the like. Residents may furnish their own rooms and have their own television sets and private phones (to be billed to the individual). Nineteen meals per week are prepared and served by the homemaker, but each resident is responsible for breakfast on the two mornings the homemaker does not work. Guests may be invited to meals, but the homemaker must be given advance notice, and the extra meals are billed. Each resident is given a key to the outside door, which is locked at night; the charge to replace a lost key is $2. One month's notice to leave is required. There are few prohibitions: no personal laundry to be hung in bathrooms; no cooking appliances (toasters, hotplates, coffee pots) permitted in bedrooms; no smoking except in the one designated area.

Included in the list of rules are the services not provided at Willow Walk: no medical care, no guarantee of lifetime care, no direct arrangement for admission to a nursing facility should such a move become necessary, no provision for extreme dietary restrictions, and a significant warning that the house does not replace the responsibility of the resident's family for emotional and financial support.

Two members of the residents' committee interview each prospective resident, who is usually accompanied by one or two family members. Candidates are accepted if they meet the age and physical requirements, express a willingness to try group living, and agree to accept the house rules. Edna, who worked with the residents' committee, was disappointed at how little attention was paid to compatibility. "That turned out to be just lip service—mostly because people weren't battering at the doors to get in, so it became impractical to be selective. We needed to fill the rooms in order to meet the mortgage payments," she said with a sigh.

"Another idea that went by the board," Carol added, "was that the residents would run the house by themselves once BLES had raised the funds, bought the building, and remodeled it. Many of the original housing-committee members thought the residents would form an association to collect rents, buy food, prepare meals, and do some of the cleaning and maintenance—or hire people to do it. But it soon became apparent that most of the people who needed the housing didn't want to or weren't capable of managing all that."

"Including me," Edna interjected. "Those were all the jobs I wanted to divest myself of when I moved out of my own place. And most of us here are pretty battle scarred and weary."

Sitting on the back porch of the house, finishing the midmorning coffee the homemaker had left for us, we could see the line of willows about 75 feet away. The newly green fronds of the trees hung over a stream, whose murmuring waters we could hear but not see, and over a stony path along its edge. Willow Creek meandered through much of the neighboring property, most of which had belonged to the first owner of the house, who had cleared the path. In time, both the path and the house had come to be called Willow Walk.

The house was built in the 1920s "like a fort," Carol said. Three stories, with a wraparound porch on three sides, it stood tall on the level lot. The stucco and timber exterior gave it an English country look. Edna characterized its style as "Victorian, with Tudor pretensions." A large and rambling house, it had many of the extras that few modern houses can afford—a library on the main floor in addition to the living room, dining room, huge kitchen and pantry, and two maids' rooms and a bath (made into an apartment for the homemaker and her husband). The library and part of the oversized living room had been converted to two bedrooms and the guest powder room into a full bathroom without seeming to diminish the common space. Four large bedrooms, two baths, and a sitting corner under the eaves made up the second floor; the third had two dormered rooms, a bathroom, and a large, low-ceilinged storeroom that could be used for one or two more bedrooms.

Carol's comment about future construction was, "If we can manage the house well and keep it full, we can go ahead with an expansion. Maybe even another house."

The house was fully occupied, and three people had signed a waiting list. The occupants, six women and two men, ranged in age from 74 to 89. Edna and another woman were church members. Two of the other women, hospital social-service-department referrals, had been waiting to move into a nursing home because they had no homes to return to after convalescence.

The fifth resident was a local appliance dealer's father who had been living in an Arizona retirement community when his wife died. Another woman had been housekeeper for a local family for over half a century; the family gradually dwindled until only the widow remained. When the widow died at age 92, her children cared for the 83-year-old housekeeper and helped her move into Willow Walk.

The second male resident was a lifelong bachelor who had been a handyman and school custodian. Though he got around well with a cane, injuries he sustained in a fall made it difficult for him to manage household tasks. The last person to move in was a beauty-salon operator who had run her business until she was 74, when a second heart attack forced her to sell it. Married and divorced twice before the age of 40, she had no children. A married sister in town had persuaded her to come to Willow Walk.

When asked how they felt about living in the house, all the residents said they were reasonably happy and much less lonely than they had been for many years. The two men were especially appreciative of the home-like atmosphere, the meals, and the companionship. The man whose son worked nearby was grateful to be close to him again. "I can hop on a bus, and in five minutes I'm at the store," he said. "It used to be my store, you know. And even though I never lived in this town, I spent a lot of years working here. It's nice to be back in familiar territory."

The women, too, liked the companionable atmosphere, but were more prone to complain about the personal habits of the others. The former housekeeper was the most tolerant. She said, "That doesn't have to be a problem. If someone annoys you, all you have to do is go into your room and shut the door. That's a privilege I didn't always have before."

A few complained about the food, but most realized that the

meals far surpassed any that could be served at a large institution. The homemaker explained that she sat down with the residents once each week so they could plan the menu for the following week together. "It's not always easy to get a consensus, but we aim to please by rotating favorite foods," she asserted good-naturedly.

Generally, the residents were grateful for the sense of safety and security that living in the house gave them. And they all liked the location, one block from the town's main street and within easy walking distance to stores, banks, churches, a library, YMCA, movie theater, park, and doctors' and dentists' offices. Buses and the railroad also are conveniently close. At the same time, each of them expressed great pleasure over the beauty and serenity of the grounds surrounding the house—the lawns, flower beds, trees, and stream.

For Edna, the location was ideal for other reasons as well. "I'm close to Carol and all my friends who still live in town. And the church is only two short blocks away, so I can go to meetings without having to depend on anyone for transportation, at least when the weather's okay."

Edna also enjoyed the freedom from household chores, as she knew she would. Her greatest disappointment stemmed from her inability to find a friend among the residents. "These are nice people, but they don't interest me. I talk to them and eat with them, but I usually feel like I'm a hundred miles away," she confessed. Other difficulties she experienced involved kitchen chore duty, getting to meals on time, and keeping her own room tidy. Kitchen chore duty was scheduled for two residents to help the homemaker set and clear the table each day. Edna almost invariably made some excuse to avoid her turn.

"She hates timetables—a very rebellious soul," Carol said. "The main problem, I think, is that she's come to this kind of living arrangement too late. If she had been able to do it two or three years ago, she might not have developed such bad habits. The way things turned out, she lived in the rooming house for two years and never did a thing except maybe rinse her coffee cup and wash her stockings."

Carol worried that her mother would be asked to leave Willow Walk. She and Betty, who was acting as administrator on a volunteer basis, had tried innumerable times to cajole Edna into being more cooperative. "We've talked to her and talked to her, but it doesn't seem to help. But Betty knows how much effort Edna put into this project. And she's assured me there's no way they're going to put her out, unless she gets a lot worse. So I have to rely on that," Carol said.

It was important to Carol that Edna remain at Willow Walk for many reasons: first, because it was so close to her own home and she needed and wanted to see her mother often, as she always had; second was the confidence of knowing Edna was in a secure, protected environment and that she, Carol, would be notified at once if anything went wrong; and third was the knowledge that, despite her aloofness, Edna needed the interaction with other people at mealtimes and whenever she felt hemmed in by the walls of her room. "The point is: she may be lonely sometimes, but at least she's not alone," Carol concluded.

"It's too bad there were no group-shared homes like this when Mother first decided she didn't want to live by herself. It would have been a lot easier for her to adapt if she had been a little younger."

Edna said something similar: "I wish I'd thought about being old when I was younger. I had at least a half-dozen friends I'd have enjoyed sharing a house with. We could have banded together and bought a house, fixed it up, maybe rented it out until we needed it. Four of them are dead now, but at least two might have lived if we were together. One fell in the tub and wasn't found for a day or so. The other died of a heart attack in the middle of the night. Maybe, if someone had been near . . . " Her voice trailed off.

"Even now," Edna continued, "if there were more places like this to choose from, I might be able to find one with more compatible people. As it is, this has come a little too late for me."

Her church's housing committee has heard Edna speak of the need for choices for a long time, and the board of BLES, Inc. has taken it to heart. Together they plan to acquire another house and convert it to a small group-shared residence like Willow Walk. Grants will be sought from county and state community-development and housing programs and from any federal funds that may become available. Community fundraising will be tried as well. The corporation, with the help of volunteers, intends to deal with only one new project at a time but anticipates continuing its work for as long as the need exists—which undoubtedly will be a long time.

Meanwhile, a grant has been obtained to pay an administrator and bookkeeper, both jobs previously handled by volunteers. Unless this salary had come through, Betty, who had just completed her master's degree program, would have been compelled to leave in search of a paying job. Because she was so well liked in addition to being competent, there was general rejoicing at BLES and at Willow Walk.

"I'm really happy to be staying," Betty exclaimed. "Community projects like this are very exciting. Oh, it may seem as if we're trying to water the desert with a thimble, considering the national housing situation. But every time a town or a city neighborhood rescues eight or ten or a dozen people from lonely, depressing, or unsafe conditions, it makes a marked improvement in many lives—the older person, his or her family, and yes, even the community that accomplishes it. So I really feel good about being part of all this."

If our society, including its older population, were to adopt this attitude of responsibility and initiative, living arrangements of many kinds would flourish. Home sharing, group-shared homes, accessory apartments, elder cottages, subsidized housing projects, and congregate and life-care communities would be commonplace, and the elderly widow or widower living alone in a house or apartment would be the rarity. For those who did stay in their own homes, there would be sufficient home-care services and home-equity financing opportunities to alleviate distress. And no one would be homeless, either, in a caring community.

Unlikely as that utopian condition may be, it is still a goal worth striving for. So keep this in mind while you and your mother or father are exploring housing options for the elderly: you are not alone, and you may be helping others as well as your own parent (even if it is just by example) when you succeed in finding a satisfactory living arrangement.

# Appendix I. State Units on Aging

ALABAMA
Commission on Aging
State Capitol
Montgomery, AL 36130
205/261-5743

ALASKA
Older Alaskans Commission
Department of Administration
Pouch C, Mail Station 0209
Juneau, AK 99811
907/465-3250

ARIZONA
Aging and Adult Administration
Department of Economic Security
1400 West Washington Street
Phoenix, AZ 85007
602/255-4446

ARKANSAS
Office of Aging and Adult Services
Department of Social and
    Rehabilitative Services
Donaghey Building, Suite 1428
7th and Main Streets
Little Rock, AR 72201
501/371-2441

CALIFORNIA
Department of Aging
1020 19th Street
Sacramento, CA 95814
916/322-5290

COLORADO
Aging and Adult Services Division
Department of Social Services
717 17th Street
P.O. Box 181000
Denver, CO 80218-0899
303/294-5913

CONNECTICUT
Department on Aging
175 Main Street
Hartford, CT 06106
203/566-3238

DELAWARE
Division on Aging
Department of Health and Social
    Services
1901 North DuPont Highway
New Castle, DE 19720
302/421-6791

DISTRICT OF COLUMBIA
Office on Aging
1424 K. Street N.W., 2d Floor
Washington, D.C. 20011
202/724-5626

FLORIDA
Program Office of Aging and Adult
    Services
Department of Health and
    Rehabilitation Services
1317 Winewood Boulevard
Tallahassee, FL 32301
904/488-8922

GEORGIA
Office of Aging
878 Peachtree Street, N.E., Room 632
Atlanta, GA 30309
404/894–5333

GUAM
Public Health and Social Services
Government of Guam
Agana, Guam 96910

HAWAII
Executive Office on Aging
Office of the Governor
335 Merchant Street, Room 241
Honolulu, HI 96813
808/548–2593

IDAHO
Office on Aging
Room 114, Statehouse
Boise, ID 83720
208/334–3833

ILLINOIS
Department on Aging
421 East Capitol Avenue
Springfield, IL 62701
217/785–2870

INDIANA
Department of Aging and Community
  Services
251 North Illinois Street
P.O. Box 7083
Indianapolis, IN 46207–7083
317/232–7006

IOWA
Department of Elder Affairs
Suite 236, Jewett Building
914 Grand Avenue
Des Moines, IA 50319
515/281–5187

KANSAS
Department of Aging
610 West Tenth
Topeka, KS 66612
913/296–4986

KENTUCKY
Division for Aging Services
Department of Human Resources
DHR Building, 6th Floor
275 East Main Street
Frankfort, KY 40601
502/564–6930

LOUISIANA
Office of Elderly Affairs
P.O. Box 80374
Baton Rouge, LA 70898
504/925–1700

MAINE
Bureau of Maine's Elderly
Department of Human Services
State House, Station 11
Augusta, ME 04333
207/289–2561

MARYLAND
Office on Aging
State Office Building
301 West Preston Street, Room 1004
Baltimore, MD 21201
301/225–1100

MASSACHUSETTS
Department of Elder Affairs
38 Chauncy Street
Boston, MA 02111
617/727–7750

MICHIGAN
Office of Services to the Aging
P.O. Box 30026
Lansing, MI 48909
517/373–8230

MINNESOTA
Board on Aging
Metro Square Building, Room 204
Seventh and Robert Streets
St. Paul, MN 55101
612/296–2544

MISSISSIPPI
Council on Aging
301 West Pearl Street
Jackson, MS 39203–3092
601/949–2070

MISSOURI
Division on Aging
Department of Social Services
P.O. Box 1337, 505 Missouri
    Boulevard
Jefferson City, MO 65102
314/751–3082

MONTANA
Community Services Division
P.O. Box 4210
Helena, MT 59604
406/444–3865

NEBRASKA
Department on Aging
P.O. Box 95044
301 Centennial Mall, South
Lincoln, NE 68509
402/471–2306

NEVADA
Division on Aging
Department of Human Resources
505 East King Street
Kinkead Building, Room 101
Carson City, NV 89710
702/885–4210

NEW HAMPSHIRE
Council on Aging
105 Loudon Road, Building 3
Concord, NH 03301
603/271–2751

NEW JERSEY
Division on Aging
Department of Community Affairs
P.O. Box 2768
363 West State Street
Trenton, NJ 08625
609/292–4833

NEW MEXICO
State Agency on Aging
224 East Palace Avenue, 4th Floor
La Villa Rivera Building
Santa Fe, NM 87501
505/827–7640

NEW YORK
Office for the Aging
New York State Plaza
Agency Building 2
Albany, NY 12223
518/474–4425

NORTH CAROLINA
Division on Aging
1985 Umpstead Drive, Kirby Building
Raleigh, NC 27603
919/733–3983

NORTH DAKOTA
Aging Services
Department of Human Services
State Capitol Building
Bismarck, ND 58505
701/224–2577

NORTHERN MARIANA ISLANDS
Office of Aging
Department of Community and
    Cultural Affairs
Civic Center, Susupe
Saipan, Northern Mariana Islands
    96950
9411; 9732

OHIO
Department on Aging
50 West Broad Street, 9th Floor
Columbus, OH 43215
614/466–5500

OKLAHOMA
Special Unit on Aging
Department of Human Services
P.O. Box 25352
Oklahoma City, OK 73125
405/521–2281

Oklahoma Department of Human
  Services
Aging Services Division
312 N.E. 28th Street
Oklahoma City, OK 73105
405/521-2327

*OREGON*
Senior Services Division
313 Public Service Building
Salem, OR 97310
503/378-4728

*PENNSYLVANIA*
Department of Aging
231 State Street
Harrisburg, PA 17101-1195
717/783-1550

*PUERTO RICO*
Gericulture Commission
Department of Social Services
P.O. Box 11398
Santurce, PR 00910
809/721-3141; 722-0225

*RHODE ISLAND*
Department of Elderly Affairs
79 Washington Street
Providence, RI 02903
401/277-2858

*SAMOA (AMERICAN)*
Territorial Administration on Aging
Office of the Governor
Pago Pago, American Samoa 96799
011/684/633-1252

*SOUTH CAROLINA*
Commission on Aging
915 Main Street
Columbia, SC 29201
803/758-2576

*SOUTH DAKOTA*
Office of Adult Services and Aging
700 North Illinois Street, Kneip
  Building
Pierre, SD 57501
605/773-3656

*TENNESSEE*
Commission on Aging
715 Tennessee Building
535 Church Street
Nashville, TN 37219
615/741-2056

*TEXAS*
Department on Aging
P.O. Box 12786 Capitol Station
1949 IH 35, South
Austin, TX 78741-3702
512/444-2727

*TRUST TERRITORY OF THE*
  *PACIFIC*
Office of Elderly Programs
Community Development Division
Government of TTPI
Saipan, Mariana Islands 96950
9335; 9336

*UTAH*
Division of Aging and Adult Services
Department of Social Services
150 West North Temple
Box 45500
Salt Lake City, UT 84145-0500
801/533-6422

*VERMONT*
Office on Aging
103 South Main Street
Waterbury, VT 05676
802/241-2400

*VIRGIN ISLANDS*
Commission on Aging
6F Havensight Mall, Charlotte Amalie
St. Thomas, VI 00801
809/774-5884

*VIRGINIA*
Department on Aging
101 North 14th Street, 18th Floor
James Monroe Building
Richmond, VA 23219
804/225-2271

*WASHINGTON*
Bureau of Aging and Adult Services
Department of Social and Health
    Services
OB–43G
Olympia, WA 98504
206/753–2502

*WEST VIRGINIA*
Commission on Aging
Holly Grove, State Capitol
Charleston, WV 25305
304/348–3317

*WISCONSIN*
Bureau of Aging
Division of Community Services
One West Wilson Street, Room 480
Madison, WI 53702
608/266–2536

*WYOMING*
Commission on Aging
Hathaway Building, Room 139
Cheyenne, WY 82002–0710
307/777–7986

# Appendix II. Affiliated State Associations, American Association of Homes for the Aging

American Association of Homes for the Aging (AAHA)
1129 20th Street NW, Suite 400
Washington, DC 20036
202/296–5960

*Alabama Association of Homes for the Aging*
c/o Kirkwood by the River
3605 Ratliff Road
Birmingham, AL 35210
205/956–4150

*Arizona Association of Homes for the Aging*
2600 N. Central Avenue, Suite 826
Phoenix, AZ 85004
602/263–1982

*California Association of Homes for the Aging*
7311 Greenhaven Drive, Suite 175
Sacramento, CA 95831
916/392–5111

*Colorado Association of Homes and Services for the Aging*
2140 S. Holly Street
Denver, CO 80222
303/759–8688

*Connecticut Association of Nonprofit Facilities for the Aged*
110 Barnes Road, P.O. Box 90
Wallingford, CT 06492
203/269–7443

*Florida Association of Homes for the Aging*
226 W. Pensacola Street, Suite 201
Tallahassee, FL 32301
904/222–3562

*Georgia Association of Homes for the Aging*
c/o Clairmont Oaks
441 Clairmont Avenue
Atlanta, GA 30030
404/378–8887

*Illinois Association of Homes for the Aging*
1151 E. Warrenville Road
Naperville, IL 60566
312/357–9340

---

For information on the Continuing Care Accreditation Commission, contact AAHA in Washington, D.C. Affiliated state associations not available in every state.

Indiana Association of Homes for the
    Aging
1251 W. 86th Street
Indianapolis, IN 46260
317/257-1115

Iowa Association of Homes for the Aging
3839 Merle Hay Road, Suite 285
Des Moines, IA 50310
515/270-1198

Kansas Association of Homes for the Aging,
    Inc.
500 Kansas Avenue
Topeka, KS 66603
913/233-7443

Kentucky Association of Homes for the
    Aging
1115 S. 4th Street, Suite 203
Louisville, KY 40203
502/587-7333

Louisiana Association of Homes for the
    Aging
2431 S. Acadian, Suite 280
Baton Rouge, LA 70808
504/928-6894

Maryland Association of Nonprofit Homes
    for the Aging
6361 Bright Plume
Columbia, MD 21044
301/740-4585

Association of Massachusetts Homes for the
    Aging
5 New England Executive Park
Burlington, MA 01803
617/272-6592

Michigan Nonprofit Homes Association
1617 E. Kalamazoo Street, Suite 2
Lansing, MI 48912
517/372-7540

Minnesota Association of Homes for the
    Aging
2221 University Avenue, S.E.
Suite 425
Minneapolis, MN 55414
612/331-5571

Missouri Association of Homes for the
    Aging
333 S. Kirkwood Road
St. Louis, MO 63122
314/821-7644

Montana Association of Homes for the
    Aging
P.O. Box 5774
Helena, MT 59604
406/728-3210

National Capital Area Association of
    Homes for the Aging
c/o Presbyterian Home
3050 Military Road, N.W.
Washington, DC 20015
202/363-8310

Nebraska Association of Homes for the
    Aging
c/o Tabitha Home
4720 Randolph Street
Lincoln, NE 68510
402/483-7671

New Jersey Association of Nonprofit Homes
    for the Aging, Inc.
CN 1
Princeton, NJ 08540
609/452-1161

New York Association of Homes and
    Services for the Aging
194 Washington Avenue, 4th Floor
Albany, NY 12210
518/449-2707

*North Carolina Association of Nonprofit
Homes for the Aging*
c/o The United Church Retirement
Home, Inc.
100 Leonard Avenue
Newton, NC 28658
704/464–8260

*North Dakota Hospital Association*
LTC General Council
312–217 First Bank of ND Building
P.O. Box 669
Grand Forks, ND 58201
701/772–4111

*Northern New England Association of
Homes and Services for the Aging*
(Maine, New Hampshire, Vermont)
c/o Jewish Home for the Aged
P.O. Box 466
Portland, ME 04112
207/772–5456

*Association of Ohio Philanthropic Homes
and Housing for the Aging*
36 W. Gay Street, Suite 712
Columbus, OH 43215
614/221–2882

*Oregon Association of Homes for the Aging*
7150 S.W. Hampton Street, Suite 206
Tigard, OR 97223
503/684–3788

*Pennsylvania Association of Nonprofit
Homes for the Aging*
3425 Simpson Ferry Road
P.O. Box 698
Camp Hill, PA 17011
717/763–5724

*Rhode Island Association of Facilities for
the Aged*
99 Hillside Avenue
Providence, RI 02906
401/351–7540

*South Carolina Association of Nonprofit
Homes for the Aging*
P.O. Box 1203
Greenwood, SC 29648
803/227–6655

*South Dakota Association of Homes for the
Aging*
c/o Luther Manor
2900 S. Lake Avenue
Sioux Falls, SD 57105
605/336–1997

*Tennessee Association of Homes for the
Aging*
c/o Cumberland View Towers
1201 Cheyenne Boulevard
Madison, TN 37115
615/868–8653

*Texas Association of Homes for the Aging*
P.O. Box 14487
Austin, TX 78761
512/458–3545

*Virginia Association of Nonprofit Homes
for the Aging*
4900 Augusta Avenue, Suite 101A
Richmond, VA 23230
804/353–8141

*Washington Association of Homes for the
Aging*
444 N.E. Ravenna Boulevard
Seattle, WA 98115
206/526–8450

*Wisconsin Association of Homes and
Services for the Aging*
7 N. Pinckney Street
Madison, WI 53703
608/255–2208

# Appendix III. State Housing Finance Agencies

*Alabama Housing Finance Authority*
State Capitol
Montgomery, AL 36130
205/261–3145

*Alaska Housing Finance Corporation*
235 E. 8th Avenue
P.O. Box 101020
Anchorage, AK 99510
907/276–5599

*Arizona Department of Commerce*
1700 West Washington
Phoenix, AZ 85007
602/255–5371

*Arkansas Development Finance Authority*
16 & Main Streets, Madison Square
    Building
P.O. Box 8023
Little Rock, AR 72203
501/371–3545

*California Housing Finance Agency*
1121 L Street, 7th Floor
Sacramento, CA 95814
919/454–4638

  *San Francisco Office*
  2351 Powell Street, Suite 501
  San Francisco, CA 94133
  415/557–2740

  *Los Angeles Office*
  5711 West Slauson Avenue
  Culver City, CA 90230
  213/736–2355

*Colorado Housing Finance Authority*
500 East Eighth Avenue
Denver, CO 80203
303/861–8962

*Connecticut Housing Finance Authority*
40 Cold Spring Road
Rocky Hill, CT 06067
203/721–9501

*Delaware State Housing Authority*
18 The Green
P.O. Box 1401
Dover, DE 19903
302/736–4263

*District of Columbia Housing Finance*
    *Agency*
1401 New York Avenue, N.W., Suite
    540
Washington, D.C. 20005
202/628–0311

*Florida Housing Finance Agency*
2571 Executive Center Circle, East
Tallahassee, FL 32301
904/488–4197

*Georgia Residential Finance Authority*
1190 West Druid Hills Drive
Suite 270, Honeywell Center
Atlanta, GA 30329
404/894–3334

*Hawaii Housing Authority*
1002 North School Street
P.O. Box 17907
Honolulu, HI 96817
808/848–3230

*Idaho Housing Agency*
760 West Myrtle
Boise, ID 83702
208/336–0161

*Illinois Housing Development Authority*
130 East Randolph Street, Suite 510
Chicago, IL 60601
312/565–5200

*Indiana Housing Finance Authority*
1 North Capitol Avenue, Suite 515
Indianapolis, IN 46204
317/232–7777

*Iowa Finance Authority*
550 Liberty Building
418 Sixth & Grand Avenue
Des Moines, IA 50309
515/281–4058

*Kansas Housing Development Corporation*
503 Kansas Avenue, 6th Floor
Topeka, KS 66603
913/357–1850

*Kentucky Housing Corporation*
1231 Louisville Road
Frankfort, KY 40601
502/564–7630

*Louisiana Housing Financing Agency*
5615 Corporate, Suite 6A
Baton Rouge, LA 70808
504/925–3675

*Maine State Housing Authority*
295 Water Street
P.O. Box 2669
Augusta, ME 04330
207/623–2981

*Maryland Community Development
   Administration*
45 Calvert Street
Annapolis, MD 21401
301/269–3161

*Massachusetts Housing Finance Agency*
50 Milk Street, 5th, 6th & 7th Floors
Boston, MA 02109
617/451–3480

*Michigan State Housing Development
   Authority*
Plaza One Building, 401 South
   Washington
P.O. Box 30044
Lansing, MI 48909
517/373–8370

*Minnesota Housing Finance Agency*
400 Sibley Street, Suite 300
St. Paul, MN 55101
612/296–5738

*Mississippi Housing Finance Corporation*
Suite 204, Dickson Building
510 George Street
Jackson, MS 39201
601/961–4514

*Missouri Housing Development
   Commission*
3770 Broadway
Kansas City, MO 64111
816/756–3790

*Montana Board of Housing*
2001 11th Avenue
Helena, MT 59620
406/444–3040

Nebraska Investment Finance Authority
Gold's Galleria, Suite 304
1033 O Street
Lincoln, NE 68508
402/477–4406

Nevada Housing Division
Department of Commerce
1050 E. William, Suite 435
Carson City, NV 89710
702/885–4257

New Hampshire Housing Finance
    Authority
9 Constitution Drive
Bedford, NH 03102

P.O. Box 5087
Manchester, NH 03108
603/472–8623

New Jersey Housing and Mortgage Finance
    Agency
CN 070, 3625 Quakerbridge Road
Trenton, NJ 08625
609/890–8900

New Mexico Mortgage Finance Authority
115 Second Street, S.W.
Albuquerque, NM 87102
505/843–6880

New York City Housing Development
    Corporation
75 Maiden Lane, 8th Floor
New York, NY 10038
212/344–8080

New York State Division of Housing and
    Community Renewal
Two World Trade Center, Room 6060
New York, NY 10047
212/488–7126

New York State Housing Finance Agency
3 Park Avenue
New York, NY 10016
212/686–9700

New York State Mortgage Loan
    Enforcement and Administration
    Corporation
11 West 42nd Street
New York, NY 10036
212/790–2400

State of New York Mortgage Agency
260 Madison Avenue, 9th Floor
New York, NY 10016
212/340–4200

North Carolina Housing Finance Agency
424 North Blount Street
P.O. Box 28066
Raleigh, NC 27611
919/733–4550

North Dakota Housing Finance Agency
1012 East Central Avenue
P.O. Box 1535
Bismarck, ND 58502
701/244–3434

Ohio Housing Finance Agency
8 East Long Street, Suite 1200
Columbus, OH 43215
614/466–7970

Oklahoma Housing Finance Agency
1140 N.W. 63rd, Suite 200
Oklahoma City, OK 73116–6519
405/848–1144

Oregon Housing Division
Department of Commerce
110 Labor & Industries Building
Salem, OR 97310–0161
503/378–1343

Pennsylvania Housing Finance Agency
2101 North Front Street
P.O. Box 8029
Harrisburg, PA 17105–8029
717/780–3800

Puerto Rico Housing Bank and Finance
    Agency
P.O. Box 345
Hato Rey, PR 00919
809/765–2537

*Puerto Rico Housing Finance Corporation*
Box 42001, Minillas Station
San Juan, PR 00940
809/725–5125

*Rhode Island Housing and Mortgage*
    *Finance Corporation*
40 Westminster Street, Suite 1700
Providence, RI 02903
401/751–5566

*South Carolina State Housing Authority*
1710 Gervais Street, Suite 100
Columbia, SC 29201
803/758–2844

*South Dakota Housing Development*
    *Authority*
221 South Central
P.O. Box 1237
Pierre, SD 57501–1237
605/773–3181

*Tennessee Housing Development Agency*
706 Church Street
Doctor's Building, Room 226
Nashville, TN 37203–5151
615/741–2473

*Texas Housing Agency*
P.O. Box 13941
Capital Station
Austin, TX 78711
512/475–0812

*Utah Housing Finance Agency*
177 East 100 South
Salt Lake City, UT 84111
801/521–6950

*Vermont Housing Finance Agency*
One Burlington Square
P.O. Box 408
Burlington, VT 05402–0408
802/864–5743

*Virgin Islands Housing Finance Authority*
P.O. Box 12029
St. Thomas, VI 00801
809/774–4481

*Virginia Housing Development Authority*
13 South 13th Street
Richmond, VA 23219
804/782–1986

*Washington State Housing Finance*
    *Commission*
710 2nd Avenue
Suite 1090, Dexter-Horton Building
Seattle, WA 98104
206/464–7139

*West Virginia Housing Development Fund*
814 Virginia Street, East
Charleston, WV 25301
304/345–6475

*Wisconsin Housing & Economic*
    *Development Authority*
One South Pinckney, Suite 500
Post Office Box 1728
Madison, WI 53701–1728
608/266–7884

*Wyoming Community Development*
    *Authority*
139 West 2nd Street, Suite 1-C
P.O. Box 634
Casper, WY 82602
307/265–0603

# Appendix IV. General Resources

## Organizations and Agencies

Administration on Aging (AoA)
U.S. Dept. of Health and Human
  Services
330 Independence Avenue SW
Washington, DC 20201

American Association of Homes for
  the Aging (AAHA) and
Continuing Care Accreditation
  Commission (CCAC)
1129 20 Street NW
Suite 400
Washington, DC 20036

American Association of Retired
  Persons (AARP)
1909 K Street NW
Washington, DC 20049

American Health Care Association
1200 15 Street NW
Washington, DC 20005

Commission on Legal Problems of the
  Elderly
American Bar Association
1800 M Street NW
Washington, DC 20036

Council of State Housing Agencies
400 N. Capital Street NW
Suite 291
Washington, DC 20001

Farmers Home Administration
  (FmHA)
South Agriculture Bldg.
14 Street & Independence Avenue SW
Washington, DC 20250

Gray Panthers
3635 Chestnut Street
Philadelphia, PA 19104

Institute for Consumer Policy
  Research
256 Washington Street
Mt. Vernon, NY 10553

Life Safety Systems, Inc.
2100 M Street NW
#305
Washington, DC 20037

Manufactured Housing Institute
Public Affairs Dept.
1745 Jefferson Davis Highway
Arlington, VA 22202

National Association of Area Agencies
  on Aging (N4A) and
National Association of State Units on
  Aging (NASUA)
600 Maryland Avenue SW
Suite 208
Washington, DC 20024

National Association of Home Care
205 C Street NE
Washington, DC 20002

National Association of Housing and
    Redevelopment Officials
2600 Virginia Avenue NW
Washington, DC 20037

National Consumers League
1522 C Street NW
Suite 406
Washington, DC 20005

National Council of Senior Citizens
925 15 Street NW
Washington, DC 20005

National Council on the Aging
    (NCOA)
600 Maryland Avenue SW
West Wing 100
Washington, DC 20024

National HomeCaring Council
235 Park Avenue South
New York, NY 10003

National Institute on Adult Day Care
Dept. P, 600 Maryland Avenue SW
West Wing 100
Washington, DC 20024

National Institute on Aging
Public Information Office
9000 Rockville Pike
Building 31, Room 5C35
Bethesda, MD 20892

National League for Nursing/
    American Public Health
    Association
10 Columbus Circle
New York, NY 10019

National Policy Center on Housing
    and Living Arrangements for Older
    Americans, University of Michigan
200 Bonistrel Boulevard
Ann Arbor, MI 48109

Older Women's League (OWL)
1325 G Street NW (LLB)
Washington, DC 20005

Share-A-Home Associations
701 Driver Avenue
Winter Park, FL 32789

# Selected Readings

## General

Dickinson, P.A. *Sun Belt Retirement*. New York: E.P. Dutton, 1983.
———. *Retirement Edens Outside the Sun Belt*. New York: E.P. Dutton, 1980.
*Employment and Volunteer Opportunities for Older People—AoA Fact Sheet*. Washington,
    D.C.: U.S. Dept. of Health and Human Services, undated.
Hemming, Roy, ed. *Finding the Right Place for Your Retirement*. New York: 50 Plus
    Guidebooks, 1983.
*Housing for a Maturing Population*. Washington, D.C.: Urban Land Institute, 1983.
*Housing Options for Older Americans*. Washington, D.C.: AARP, 1985.
Irwin, Robert. *The $125,000 Decision*. New York: McGraw-Hill, 1981.
Lawton, M. Powell, and Sally Hoover, eds. *Community Housing Choices for the El-
    derly*. New York: Springer, 1981.

Musson, Noverre. *The National Directory of Retirement Residences: Best Places to Live When You Retire.* New York: Frederick Fell, 1973.

*Options for Living Arrangements: Housing Alternatives for the Elderly.* New York: National Council of Jewish Women, 1980.

*Protecting Your Housing Investment,* HUD–346–PA(7). Washington, D.C.: U.S. Dept. of Housing and Urban Development, October 1980.

Shattuck, Alfred. *The Greener Pastures Relocation Guide: Finding the Best States for You.* Englewood Cliffs, N.J.: Prentice-Hall, 1984.

Sumichrast, M., R.G. Shafer, and M. Sumichrast. *Planning Your Retirement Housing.* Mount Prospect, Ill.: AARP/Scott Foresman & Co., 1984.

*The Older American's Guide to Housing and Living Arrangements.* Mt. Vernon, N.Y.: Institute for Consumer Policy Research, 1984.

*Woodall's Retirement and Resort Communities Directory.* Highland Park, Ill.: Woodall's Publishing Company, published annually.

*Your Home, Your Choice: A Workbook for Older People and Their Families.* Washington, D.C.: AARP with the Federal Trade Commission, 1985.

## Chapter 2. Group-Shared Homes

Day-Lower, Dennis. *Shared Housing for Older People: A Planning Manual for Group Residences.* Philadelphia: Shared Housing Resource Center, 1983.

*Innovative Options in Elderly Housing: A Manual for Local Action.* Aetna Life and Casualty Co., February 1982. Can be obtained from Connecticut Dept. on Aging (see address in appendix I).

Murray, Priscilla. *Shared Homes: A Housing Option for Older People.* Washington, D.C.: International Center for Social Gerontology, 1975.

*National Directory of Shared Housing Programs for Older People.* Philadelphia: Shared Housing Resource Center, 1983.

Streib, G., E. Folts, and M.A. Hilker. *Old Homes, New Families: Shared Living for the Elderly.* New York: Columbia University Press, 1984.

## Chapter 3. Congregate and Life-Care Communities

*A Consumer Guide to Life Care Communities.* Washington, D.C.: National Consumers League, 1985.

Carlin, Vivian F., and Ruth Mansberg. *If I Live to Be 100 . . . Congregate Housing for Later Life.* West Nyack, N.Y.: Parker Publishing, 1984.

Raper, A.T., ed. *National Continuing Care Directory.* Mount Prospect, Ill.: AARP/Scott Foresman, 1984.

*Consumers' Guide to Independent Living for Older Americans: The Life Care Alternative.* Doylestown, Pa.: Life Care Society of America, 1979.

*Continuing Care Retirement Community: A Guidebook for Consumers.* Washington, D.C.: American Association of Homes for the Aging, 1983.

*The Directory of Retirement Communities in the U.S.* Ann Arbor, Mich.: National Policy Center on Housing and Living Arrangements, Institute of Gerontology, University of Michigan, 1981.

## Chapter 4. Home Sharing

Dobkin, Leah. *Shared Housing for Older People: A Planning Manual for Match-up Programs.* Philadelphia: Shared Housing Resource Center, 1983.
*Is Homesharing for You? A Self-Help Guide for Homeowners and Renters.* Philadelphia: Shared Housing Resource Center, 1983.

## Chapter 4. ECHO Housing

*ECHO Housing Slide/Tape Presentation and Fact Sheet.* Washington, D.C.: AARP, 1983.
Guion, Edward. "Elder Cottages: A New Feature on the Housing Horizon." *Aging*, special issue on housing (December 1983–January 1984).
Shepherd, Paul. "Granny Flats May Be the Answer." *Human Development News*, U.S. Dept. of Health and Human Services (August–September 1982).

## Chapter 4 and Chapter 5. Accessory Apartments

Hare, P.H., and S. Dwight. *Accessory Apartments: Using Surplus Space in Single Family Houses.* Chicago: American Planning Association, 1981.
Hare, P. H. *Creating an Accessory Apartment.* New York: McGraw-Hill, 1986.

## Chapter 4 and Chapter 5. Home-Equity Conversion

Scholen, Ken. *Unlocking Home Equity: New Ideas for Homeowners—Conference Proceedings.* Madison, Wis.: Wisconsin Bureau on Aging Reverse Equity Mortgage Project, Dept. of Health and Social Services, 1979.
*Turning Home Equity into Income for Older Homeowners.* Washington, D.C.: U.S. Senate Special Committee on Aging, July 1982.

## Chapter 5. Home Care and Day Care

*A Handbook about Care in the Home.* Washington, D.C.: AARP Fulfillment D955, 1982.
*All about Home Care: A Consumers Guide.* New York: National HomeCaring Council, 1983.
Schwarz, Richard. "Day Care Center Brings New Perspective to Mount Vernon Elderly." *Aging* (March–April 1983).

## Chapter 6. Condominiums

Le Croissette, Dennis. *Condominium Living: Your Guide to Buying and Living in a Condominium.* Montrose, Calif.: Young-Husband Co., 1980.
*Questions and Answers about Condominiums: What to Ask before You Buy.* Pueblo, Colo.: U.S. Dept. of Housing and Urban Development, Consumer Information Center, 1974.

## Chapter 7. Home Safety

Raschko, Bettyann B. *Housing Interiors for the Disabled and Elderly.* New York: Van Nostrand Reinhold, 1982.

*Safety for Older Consumers: Home Safety Check List.* Washington, D.C.: U.S. Consumer Product Commission, January 1985.

# Notes

## Introduction

1. *A Profile of Older Americans: 1985* (Washington, D.C.: American Association of Retired Persons and Administration on Aging, U.S. Dept. of Health and Human Services, 1985), 1.
2. *Aging America: Trends and Projections—1985–86 Edition* (Washington, D.C.: U.S. Senate Special Committee on Aging with AARP, Federal Council on the Aging, and AoA, 1985), 22.

## Chapter 1. One Widow's Dilemma

1. *Profile of Older Americans*, 1.
2. *Aging America*, 8.

## Chapter 3. For the Rest of My Life—Or Almost

1. Evelyn W. Hale, "Life in a Life Care Community," *Hot Flash* (State University of New York, Stony Brook) 4 (Winter 1984): 3.
2. *Analysis of the 1981 Subsidized Housing Survey* (Trenton, N.J.: State Dept. of Community Affairs, Division on Aging, May 1982).
3. John Herbers, "Program to House Aged Facing New Questions," *New York Times*, 17 January 1986.
4. William Gordon, "Congregate Housing Helps Dependent Elderly Keep Their Independence," Newark (N.J.) *Star Ledger*, 30 April 1986.

## Chapter 4. Your Place and Mine

1. Maxine Livingstone, ed., *Report on Forum III—Housing for the Retired* (Washington, D.C.: Federal National Mortgage Association, 1979) 36.
2. *Profile of Older Americans*, 4.

3. Vivian F. Carlin and Ruth Mansberg, *If I Live to Be 100 . . . Congregate Housing for Later Life* (W. Nyack, N.Y.: Parker Publishing, 1984).
4. Edward Guion, "Elder Cottages: A New Feature on the Housing Horizon," *Aging* (special issue/housing, AoA), December 1983–January 1984.
5. *ECHO Housing Fact Sheet* (AARP, undated).

## Chapter 5. Home, Sweet Home

1. Phyllis Myers, *Aging in Place: Strategies to Help Elderly in Revitalizing Neighborhoods* (Washington, D.C.: The Conservation Foundation, 1982) 21–25.
2. *Profile of Older Americans*, 4, 11.
3. *Aging America*, 2–4.
4. *Turning Home Equity into Income for Older Homeowners* (Washington, D.C.: U.S. Senate Special Committee on Aging, undated).
5. *Federal Programs for Older Persons* (Trenton, N.J.: State Dept. of Community Affairs, Division on Aging, January 1986) 29–32.
6. Susan C. Ficke, ed., *An Orientation to the Older Americans Act* (Washington, D.C.: National Association of State Units on Aging, July 1985) 53.
7. *Your Home, Your Choice: A Workbook for Older People and Their Families* (Washington, D.C.: AARP with Federal Trade Commission, 1985) 8.
8. Donna Leigh, "When a Community Cares," *Parade Magazine*, 13 July 1986, 16.
9. "In-Home Alarm System," *Parent Care* (University of Kansas Gerontology Center) 1 (May–June 1986) 1.
10. Joan Whitlow, "Surrogates Filling an Expanding Gap in Care for Elderly," Newark (N.J.) *Sunday Star Ledger*, 5 January 1986.
11. "Tapes Surpass Braille in Popularity for Blind," *New York Times*, 20 July 1986.

## Chapter 6. Surveying the Field

1. Vivian F. Carlin and Dennis Richardson, "Effect of Changing Life Patterns in Retirement Villages" (paper presented to Gerontological Society of America, Portland, Ore., October 1974).
2. Annette Winter, "Living in the Slow Lane," *Modern Maturity*, February–March 1986. 93–96.
3. *Profile of Older Americans*, 4.
4. Ibid., 3.
5. Beverly Hoeffer, "Predictors of Life Outlook of Older Single Women" (paper presented to Gerontological Society of America, New Orleans, Louis.: November 1985) 3.
6. Carlin and Mansberg, *If I Live to Be 100*, 125–46.
7. *Journal of Housing for the Elderly* (Spring–Summer 1983): 90.
8. Laura A. Spitz, "Life Care Communities," *NCL Bulletin* (National Consumers League) 45 (November–December 1983): 1.
9. Carol A. Schreter and Lloyd A. Turner, "Sharing and Subdividing Private Market Housing," *The Gerontologist* 26, no. 2 (1986): 81.

10. Jane Porcino, "Intergenerational Shared Housing," *Hot Flash* 4 (Winter 1984): 3.
11. *Aging America*, 35.
12. Ibid., 37.

## Chapter 7. What's Your Pleasure? And How to Find It

1. Barbara Silverstone and Helen Kandel Hyman, *You and Your Aging Parent* (New York: Pantheon Books, 1976) 168. Copyright by the authors.
2. "Your Personal Guide to Retirement Housing," *Harvest Years*, September 1972.
3. Annette Winter, "What Should I Do? *Modern Maturity*, August–September 1986, 82.
4. Alan S. Oser, "New Ideas for Elderly Tested in Jersey Shore County," *New York Times* 15 June 1986, Real Estate section.

## Chapter 8. Who Are the Elderly?

1. Robert N. Butler, *Breaking Images: The Media and Aging*, monograph no. 3 (New York: Columbia University School of Journalism, 1979) 1.
2. Unless otherwise stated, the statistics in this chapter are from *A Profile of Older Americans* and *Aging America: Trends and Projections*. Please see notes 1 and 2 under *Introduction* for full references.
3. "Marital Status and Living Arrangements," *Current Population Reports* (Washington, D.C.: U.S. Bureau of the Census, March 1981) 81.
4. *Near poor* is defined as income between the poverty level and 125 percent of this level. (*Profile of Older Americans*, 10.)
5. *America in Transition: An Aging Society—Developments in Aging*, vol. 1, chap. 1 (Washington, D.C.: U.S. Senate Special Committee on Aging, 1983).
6. "Three Budgets for a Retired Couple," *Bureau of Labor Statistics News* (Washington, D.C.: U.S. Department of Labor, 1982) 2.
7. *Journal of Housing for the Elderly*, Spring–Summer 1983, 90.
8. *1981 Annual Housing Survey*, vol. C. (Washington, D.C.: U.S. Bureau of the Census, 1983).
9. *Journal of Housing*, 90.
10. Gordon Streib, Edward Folts, and Mary Anne Hilker, *Old Homes, New Families: Shared Living for the Elderly* (New York: Columbia University Press, 1984), 24–25.
11. M. G. Kover, "Health of the Elderly and Use of Health Services," *Public Health Reports*, January–February 1977.
12. Elaine M. Brody, "Social, Economic, and Environmental Issues Relating to Aging, With Some Thoughts About the 'Women in the Middle,' " *Aging: Research and Perspectives* 41.
13. Lloyd Turner and Eglute Mangum, *Report on the Housing Choices of Older Americans* (Washington, D.C.: National Council on Aging, March 1982) vi.
14. Elizabeth M. Markson, ed., *Older Women* (Lexington, Mass.: Lexington Books, 1983) 232.

15. "Interdisciplinary Research on the Service of the Aged," *Geriatrics* 30, nos. 10, 11, 12 (1975).

16. *Aging America*, 91.

17. Karen Schaar, "Vermont: Getting through the Adult Years," *APA Monitor* (American Psychological Association) September–October 1978, 29.

18. Elaine M. Brody and Claire B. Schoonover, "Patterns of Parent Care When Adult Daughters Work and When They Do Not," *The Gerontologist* 26 (August 1986) 373–380.

19. Arlie Hochschild, *The Unexpected Community* (Berkeley: University of California Press, 1973).

20. Carlin and Mansberg, *If I Live to Be 100.*

21. Turner and Mangum, *Report on Housing Choices*, vii.

22. Sandra C. Howell, "Determinants of Housing Choice: Perceptions and Actions" (paper presented to International Congress on Gerontology, New York, July 1985).

23. *Housing Choices for Older Americans* (Washington, D.C.: AARP, 1983) 11.

# Index

# About the Authors

VIVIAN F. CARLIN is a consulting gerontologist specializing in housing and preretirement planning. Coauthor of *If I Live to Be 100 . . . Congregate Housing for Later Life*, Dr. Carlin recently retired from a position as supervisor of the Office of Planning and Policy Analysis of the New Jersey State Division on Aging. On the division staff for 15 years, she developed such new programs as Elderly Home Conversion (the first in the U.S.) and Congregate Housing Services (the first in New Jersey and third in the nation). She has presented papers and led training sessions at international, national, and regional gerontology conferences. Dr. Carlin received her Ph.D. in social policy/gerontology from Rutgers University and is also a certified psychologist.

RUTH MANSBERG is a freelance writer and coauthor of *If I Live to Be 100*. She has many years of experience as a newspaper and magazine editor and has written numerous articles on housing, health care, and a variety of other subjects. She is a graduate of Hunter College, New York City, and a member of The Authors Guild.

Other important lifestyle titles from

## Lexington Books

(As seen on the **Modern Maturity** TV show)
*To Be Old and Sad: Understanding Depression in the Elderly*
*Nathan Billig, M.D.*

"Of all the problems that older people face, depression is surely one of the most complex. A web of poorly understood factors, including fears of death and loss as well as biological and life changes, sometimes produce a despairing outlook in the elderly. But according to geriatric psychiatrist Nathan Billig, depression among this age group . . . is neither inevitable nor irreversible. . . . Billig discusses how older people can fight back. . . This book includes a clear description of depression (what it is as well as what it is not) and an explanation of the difference between depression and dementia. It also summarizes useful information for the families of older depressed people."—*Psychology Today*      "Written primarily as a guide to help family members cope with a parent, spouse or relative who is suffering from depression, this also provides warning signals that may help depression sufferers themselves to recognize their illness and seek treatment."—*Kirkus Reviews*      0-669-12279-3      **$8.95 (paper)**

*Sexual Health in Later Life*
*Thomas H. Walz and Nancee S. Blum*

This book is a sensitively written, myth-shattering guide to one of the most critical facets of our lives. In clear, everyday language, it explains the value of sex after sixty and discusses the effects of aging, chronic illness, medical treatments, and mental states on sexual desires and capacities. Contains a self-evaluation test especially designed by the authors for this book. "A frank, easy-to-read book aimed at older people as well as their families and health practitioners."—*Iowa City Press-Citizen*   0-669-14599-8   **$9.95 (paper)**

**Available in finer bookstores everywhere. Or call (toll-free):**
**1-800-235-3565. Or use the convenient form below.**

| | |
|---|---|
| Name _____ | Card Number _____ |
| Street _____ | Expiration date _____ |
| City _____ State _____ Zip _____ | Signature _____ |
| Phone _____ | _____ I prefer to pay by check or money order. (Please include the price of the book(s) plus $2.00 for postage and handling.) |
| _____ Please charge the book(s) to my credit card: | |
| _____ VISA_____ Mastercard_____ AmericanExpress | |

**Allow 6-8 weeks for delivery.** *Guarantee:* **If you are not satisfied with the book for any reason, return it within 30 days for a full refund.**
**Send this order with payment to: Lexington Books • 125 Spring Street • Lexington, MA 02173**